I0902072

PRAISE FOR *NO SILENCE IN THE AFTERLIFE*

No Silence in the Afterlife broke my heart and healed it. Abou Farman gifts us a language that once belonged to our ancestors and to their ancestors, who exist as cosmos and earth, born up as we each were from ancient oceans. In this book, love is not love but rather a poetics of elemental earthly and fleshly beingness. Here language is a complex reciprocity—one magnet/ism—which peripheries us together, compels or repels us, beckons or scatters us, in whatever absence and presence a body was, is, and becomes of the world and its labyrinthine energies, ancient and futuristic, dangerous and static. The beloved's body becomes your body, and your body becomes the beloved's body, and each of those bodies become our ancestors' bodies, and our bodies of the coming mornings—a little lost, a little gone, arriving and receiving, and in these flickering states fully present, the ecstatic as a circle of cells that multiply us into and out of one another's lives. The "I of you" as they call it, each of us inciting or reorganizing the other's "desire to last."

—**NATALIE DIAZ**, Pulitzer Prize-winning poet

Abou Farman mourns the loss of his beloved as she crosses into the invisible. He sends sonic and poetic gestures after her into the after-states and the cosmos, linguistically exploring the transparent realm as testament to his organic contact with what persists here, on this side, with him. Farman's words merge with an ironic glow, alive with his adamantine spirit, vibrating with luster, active within higher verbal forms, kinetic in spirit, and self-scrolling onwards as a living enigma.

—**WILL ALEXANDER**, American Book Award-winning poet

NO SILENCE IN THE AFTERLIFE

NO SILENCE IN THE AFTERLIFE

ABOU FARMAN

LEONOR CARABALLO

ORIGINAL ARTWORK BY
CARABALLO-FARMAN, SARA FLORES & ABOU FARMAN

NOEMI PRESS

Published by Noemi Press, Inc. A Nonprofit Literary Organization.
www.noemipress.org

Cover & Book Design by co•im•press
Cover Photo by caraballo-farman

ISBN: 978-1-955992-72-5

APPEARING

Nuclear Magnetic • 7
Life Time Risk • 17
Resonance • 22
Tumor • 29
Mold • 34
What the Tumor Said • 39

DISAPPEARING

Decay • 45
Absence • 46
Cut • 47
Immortality • 57
Survival • 63
Aneasthetic • 69
Shit • 80
Last Question • 87

REAPPEARING

No Silence • 95
Orphic • 98
Miscellaneous Wonder • 101
Leaky • 107
Others Dream • 109
Cry • 113
Mourn • 120
Mourn II • 127
Utterances • 130
Presence • 132
Presence (Again) • 137

APPEARING

1.40 am
January 24, 2015

So now

how

must I live

every day

with

you?

NUCLEAR MAGNETIC

Three or four mysterious forces without which
we would not be here

none of us

without which
the universe
would not have come together

nothing

so

they must be there

they must always have been

there

without which

nothing

none of us

Of all things

—the mastodons, the stallions, the candles, the mascara, the mammaries, the mutations, the vibrators, the medications, the hair, the cameras, the indoor plants and the cedar wood, the suede shoes, the eyes, the wild bottomless eyes, the moon in them, their precision, the anger and fits, the bunions, the strength of your grip, the smell of horses in your nostrils, the question mark in your ears, the labyrinths of silence in your day, the laughter too, its bigness, and the sad tombak of your heart, all reverberation—

of what made you up,
there were also some four octillion seven hundred septillion
and one or two hydrogen protons

to a great extent
you were made up of hydrogen protons

everyone is

For a period
there was nothing
more fundamental

I proton

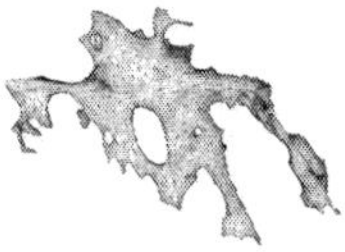

You proton

now there are three quarks[i]

quark
quark
quark

the seabirds call[iii]

No one knows what a quark is
or what they are up to
or what they might be made up of, if they are made up

of anything

the way we are made up

held together by three or four mysterious forces[ii]

and dark energy

that thirteen point eight billion years ago

give or take

made particle soup.

Time slipped by.

No one saw it coming.

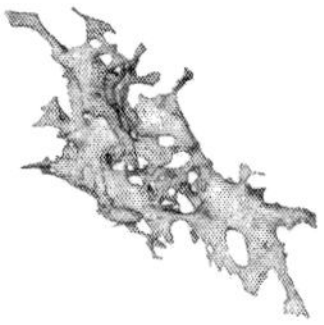

Four hundred thousand years later[iv]

protons got together with electrons[v]
to make the first atoms
out of the force of attraction[vi]

out of love[viii]

and a promise

they
would not be separated, even when forced, even at a distance,[vii] even as photons, even on a dead cat's whisker, even when in Tibet, even when dust on a butterfly wing,[ix] even in storms, floods, fires, eruptions, in ashes even, even in hate, at the end, ever,   even   never

then   gases

and it's a blur

supernovas gamma ray bursts electromagnetic waves planets fire earth mountains water cells sugar DNA bacteria whales and fish trees flowers petrodactyls turtles snakes DMT mosquitoes yellow bees red cardinals lions baboons Neanderthals tumors you and me and nuclear bombs and Nuclear Magnetic Resonance Imaging machines

and   ooooooph   what a different order to come into

under the skin
the cosmic goings on
going on

all the beginnings held

lifelikenonlife

in us

protons spinning
with the giddiness of those who come out of nowhere
with moment
with charge
with energy
with radiation

your body

passed down unseen
through
vulvic folds of time

this vastness
you feel acutely

when you are given[x]
two years

to live

two years  to die

two two two two

count it in years then count it in months days hours—two— minutes—two—time that's left and time that's passed are part of the same body of time—two—this way and that

in that kind of time grammar falls apart

we make up the tense of survival

the future terminal[xi]

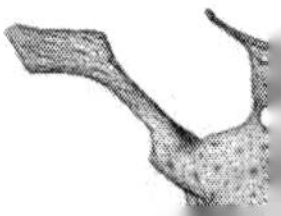

Prophecy

makes a new kind of body

places
in it the ticking[xii]

Ya

it comes down to this

time

you in it   it beyond you

until you learn
how to walk
on the other side of time[xiii]

LIFE TIME RISK

Zero one zero zero zero one

down the bleep wire of a machine
judgment
smudged
on fax paper
bad copy
of a copy
about a bad copy

It said,
every beginning is an accident.

It said,
the Patient is a 36-year-old woman
with biopsy-proven
invasive
lobular
carcinoma
of her left breast
and a family history
of premenopausal breast cancer.

mutations
in the signs
r
mutations in fate

It said,
the biopsy-proven carcinoma
corresponds to a 1.8 cm irregular enhancing mass at 5 to 6 o'clock.[xiv]

digital genetic
positive negative

It said,
tick tock.

appeardisappear
saynotsay

It said,
the specimen is fresh
the mass mammographically occult
the breast young, the tissue dense
the axillary tail dressed in orange
the nipple tagged red.

this breast I thought I knew

It said,
deleterious mutation.

lullaby the spirits

It said,
somewhere between base pair 31,787,616
and base pair 31,871,804
on the long arm of chromosome 13
a tumor suppressor gene whose job was to repair
damaged DNA and regulate the wild
cell divisions
failed.

cellular gobbledygook is not nonsense
not good sense not innocence[xv]
just that much closer to the end[xvi]

The abstractions are too concrete
155,000 human beings die every day
90 billion homo sapiens are dead and gone already
since the rise of homo sapiens
millions of species going going gone forever
we walk in their dust
those who came before us
we spin their protons
their genes R us
we are the formations of their information
we are the scribes and scribes make mistakes—
none of this could've unfolded without those mistakes.

Still, what the fuck does it take to get A C T and G right?

Where was the autocorrect?
you joked.
Ashkenazi blood is bad blood,
the geneticist joked back.

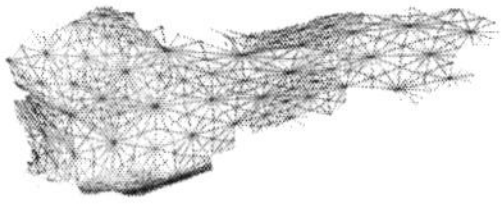

history is probability
ethnicity a medium of transmission for 3 billion base pairs
family the intensification of errors

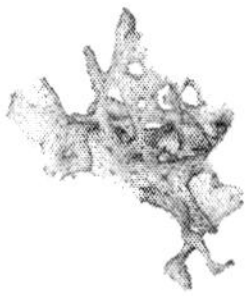

When Alfredo crossed the ocean and made money
he figured that's mainly what he would pass down—
cows land farmworkers grain bread baskets Monsanto soybean eye
color skin shade jet fuel off-shore accounts etiquette horse saddles.

the law of bunions and the law of banks
stamped differently upon each class

with your mistakes and mutations

come pass through me

be my north

be my error

RESONANCE

A magnetic field ten thousand times stronger than the earth's

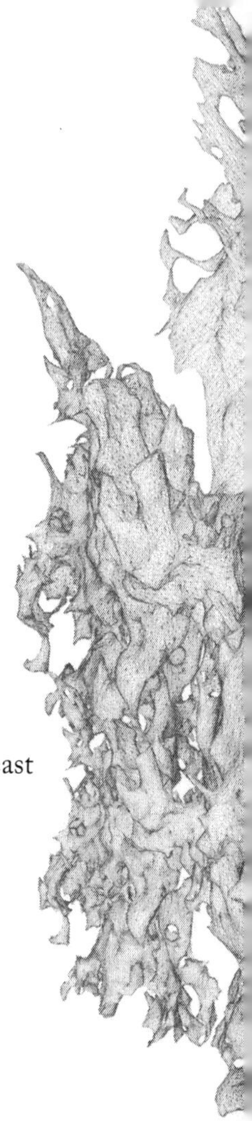

reveals

the little tumor   inside   your breast

magnetic planet
magnetic body
magnetic field
magnetic machine

an order necessary
for imaging

for the wild has no image

hence wild

From inside the handbook of how our insides appear:

1. A Magnetic Resonance Imaging machine can make an image of your lightless interior by tapping into the power of hydrogen protons in all your organs and tissue.
2. That big tunnel you get slipped into is a magnetic coil of superconducting copper wire creating a field about 1.5 tesla.
3. Because protons from the early universe are electromagnetically susceptible,[xvii] the magnetic field lines up all your hydrogen protons in one direction.
4. A radio transmitter hits them with a radio signal of 10 to 100 MHz. This is the resonant frequency[xviii] of hyrdrogen protons in your body. As a result, all your hydrogen protons bump up one energy state with the resonance of that frequency.
5. When the radio transmitter stops, the hydrogen protons flip back to their energy state of origin, but at different rates: they flip faster in the tumor, slower in the flesh. As they release, they emit their own radio signal.
6. A receiver built into the MRI machine picks up that signal.[xix] The image of your interior is made of all those radio signals emitted at different rates by hydrogen protons in your body.

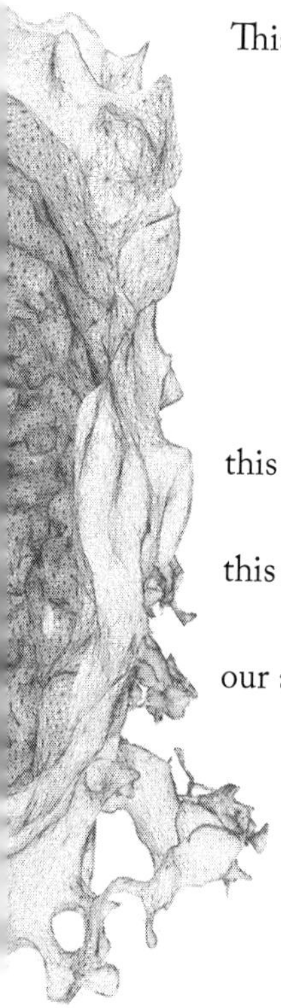

This is   your body   we are talking about

all magnetic, nuclear, oscillating,
transmitting radio frequencies
like there was no tomorrow

this is us, our cells behaving this way

this is us and the universe and our forces and charges and fields

our ability to absorb each other

and

emit

signals

this is us below biology

your protons aroused to a higher spin rate[xx]

amplifying   the recognition

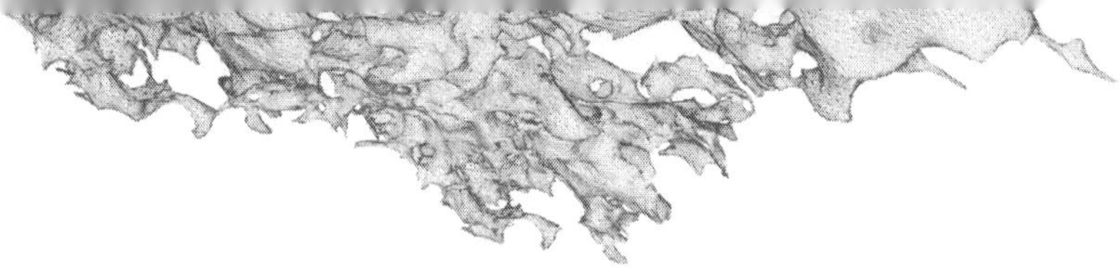

you flip my state

turn my moment

this you
is
this me

THIS
~~AND~~
THIS

you ping me I ping you radio me radio you bump me bump you jolt
me jolt you spin me spin you miss me miss you

yes you, yes me, yes you, yes me, yes yes yes yes yes yes
yes you

this much is science[xxi]

until then
we didn't know you were a radio

didn't know you could
hiss and quack
through all these states
of emission[xxii]

YOU
~~IS~~
ME

didn't know the body
had so many miracles in it

or that we needed so many more

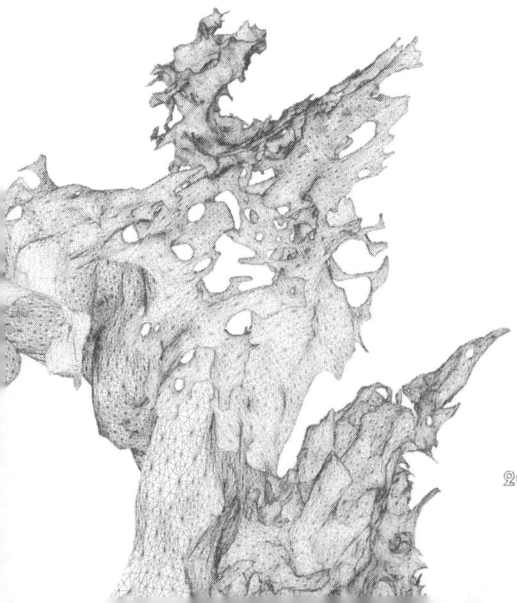

The Armenian inventor who figured it out
named his first machine Indomitable.

Of the way he came to his invention, he wrote:

"There was only one rational explanation: God."[xxiii]

God or not God, if we accept physics' story of the universe, we also would have to say at least this much:

the technology of our body
is the technology of the
universe[xxiv]

:

hydrogen protons
whirling
in electromagnetic madness

I want to ask the radiologists,[xxv] physicists, oncologists, technicians if they know how we came to this.

We, the protons, how did we come to fear? to envy?
how did one proton feel superior to another? how did we protons come to know faith? illness? injustice? death? time? hate? verbs? beauty? how did we come to know questions? to know when to ask why? and when when? when did we the protons come to think we know what the future holds?

or what
a proton is[xxvi]

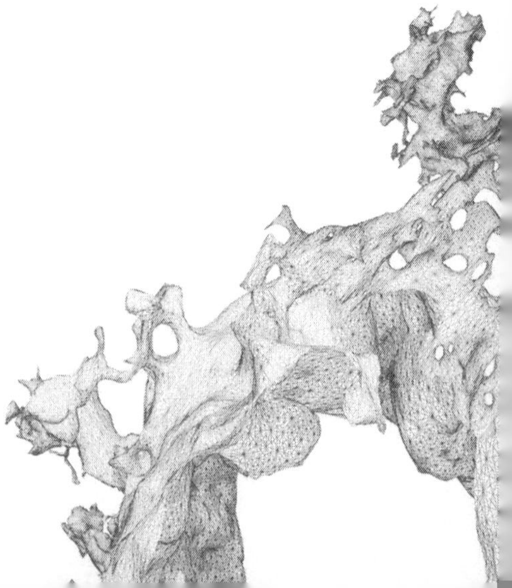

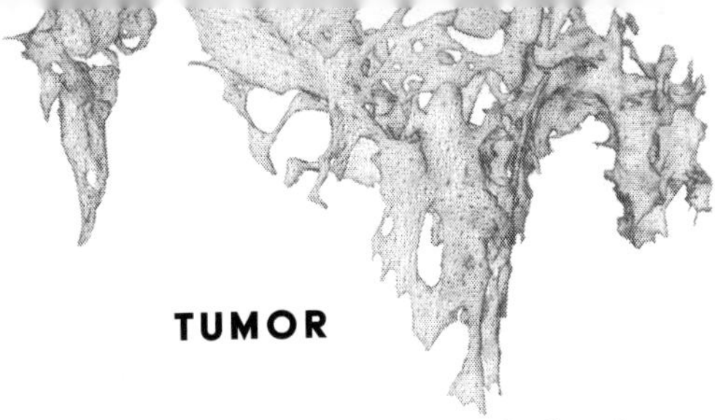

TUMOR

The way your eyes lifted and your woodpecker mind kept tapping buts

but what is a tumor?
but but but what
does it look like?
but has it no image?
none?
but?

It is fall

everything red and orange across the northeast

the landscape of bruised skin and biopsies.

The network transmits Ms Lovely's voice from Aetna:

the diagnosis code 174.4 is for malignancy of the upper quadrant of
the female breast
the procedure code is 38972
SENTINEL NODE BIOPSY code 38525 does not need
pre-approval

if you do radio you reduce the risk by 3%
add 5% for chemo,
30% for tamoxifen but over 10 years
and a few half points for diet.

The numbers play you
a tumor makes the rest of life subject to a count

it's a matter of probabilities, a matter of maybes, maybe-nots,
maybe-not-mes, maybe-i-am-that-other-part-of-risk, maybe-i-
have-more-time, maybe-i-have-more-luck, maybe-they-don't-know-
from-statistics, maybe-i-count-better, count-more, maybe-I-Am-
A-Survivor, maybe-i-will-be-next-year-too, next-month, maybe,
maybe-not

a tumor is the hollow
of hope dug up and sliced
& sent over to pathology
to calculate the rate of your body's betrayal

a tumor is a bunch of cells declaring independence, mutants in mutiny
refusing death

a tumor yields knowledge
spreads statistically
gives off data
enters a database
and thus do you come to know
your chances
if you cut off your left breast.

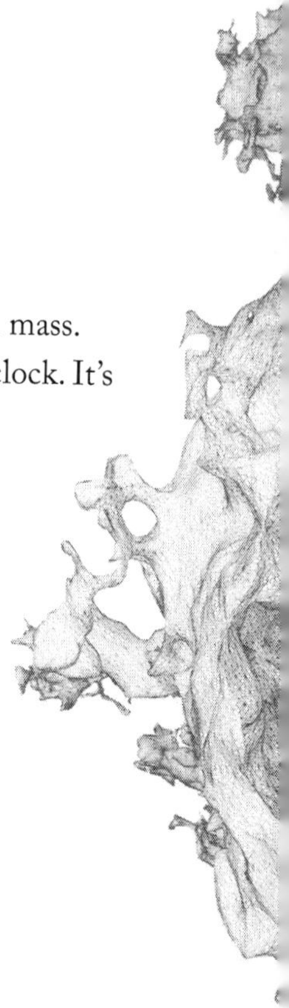

It's pea-sized. It's the size of a golf ball. Or a turkey egg. It's a mass. It's hard. It's round. It's old. It's ancient. It's occult. It's at 5 o'clock. It's pink.

It's pink?
Like a ribbon.
Like hope.
Like a teddy bear.
Like Barbie.
Like a Sharpie. Like BMW. Like a Prayer.
Like courage.
Like a super stickie.
Like Avon.
Like Revlon.
Like NFL linebackers
in October.

Life proliferating
sooner or later is a tumor.[lxi]

Cells, more cells. Calcifications. Doctors. Sonographers.
Mammographers. Radiologists. Oncologists. MRI technicians.
Shelley. Knives. Sharpies. Needles. 5 centimeter Kopans hookwires.
Stereotactic biopsies. The long arm of chromosome 13. BRCA
proteins. X-Rays. MRIs. Scans. Warm compresses. Genetic counselors.
Magnetized atoms. Wigs. Lymph nodes. Padded bras. 3D software.
Pink teddy bears. Hydrogen protons. Shamans. Fear.
This coming together is the tumor.

A tumor means   wasted time

                                        and time not to be wasted

time passing too slow and time passing too fast but always passing

passing with the sound of a shadow passing through a shadow.

The way your eyes suddenly lifted.

The way the oncologist looked back.

The way you said, I want to see it.

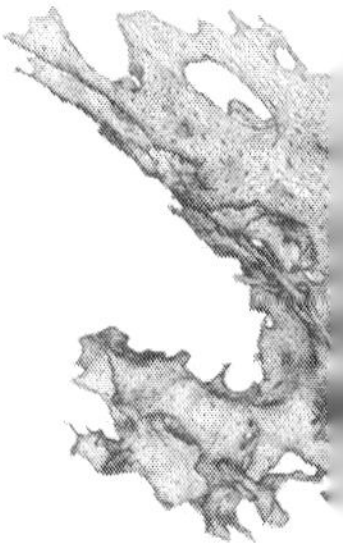

MOLD

The cells multiplied
made a tumor
my body its mold.

A mold is one thing shaped around another
one matter poured around another
sealed, understanding the parts
figuring the split lines
two bodies wrapped around each other
testing their geometries
seeing how they fit
snug airtight breathless
one
the inverse
of the other
the heart and its hollow
the blow and its trauma
love and need
the character and its actor
the parent and the child
the shoe in the snow
the shoe out of the snow
the now out of its prior.

A mold is the shape of the understanding of a shape
a place to hold something tight
a place from which it must be removed
to become again
        the thing, one more of itself
and also of something else one more.

A word is a mold
wraps itself around things
leaf around leaf
glass around glass
cancer around tumor
absence around presence.

When we got together, we got together a new language
molding us. Words grown over the years in each one
expanding into new corners.

When you wanted to make love, you'd ask, "You want to visit me?"
And when I embarrassed you in public, you said, "Temer o ridículo!"

When we bought a house and tried to make it a home,
we constructed us in a new language
of compound and joint tape, R-19 and single-pole dimmers.
For a long time, coming back to it on the train,
we couldn't say we were going "home," until one day,
when words like jig saw and caulk had faded,
we did, we said we are going home.

A turn in life builds its own language
to outline the shape of new things.

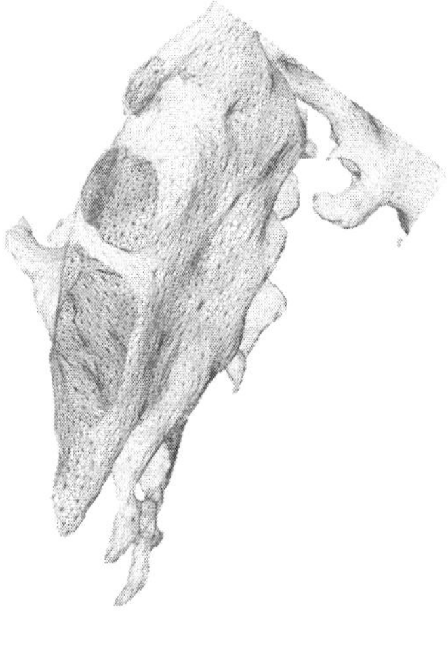

In the time of the tumor,
our lexicon spanned across lobular and lymph node
to creatinine and potassium and oncologist. We wanted to use them
only
till they diminished
till we could look up and see other things ahead, and say,

we are going home.

How many times on the way back
from the hospital
our hopes dilated
did we say that?
How many times did I say it to myself
and what is praying
but this periphrasis of hope, this muttering
over and over on a platform waiting
for the train home, whispers leaving the body?
How many times did I murmur, it is just this
tumor and nothing more, nothing escaped, nothing in the
microcalcifications
nothing in that blown out node of light the radiologist called a ghost
no nothing
for the blue striped gowns are clean, pressed
the wire localization precise, the anesthesia worked like a charm
the surgeon's knife was sharp
the margins wide and clean, the lymph nodes free
no nothing can escape?

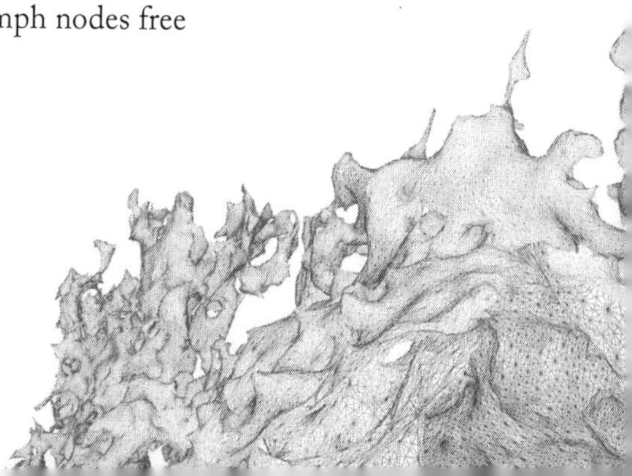

In the waiting room,

the white Presbyterian bricks, the Italian coffee machine
the red-head intern sliding up and down the aisles like a bell boy
calling "family of Desiderio," "family of Connaghie,"
while I waited alone there, the family of Leonor

repeating to myself 

we'll be going home

breasts missing

but home

.

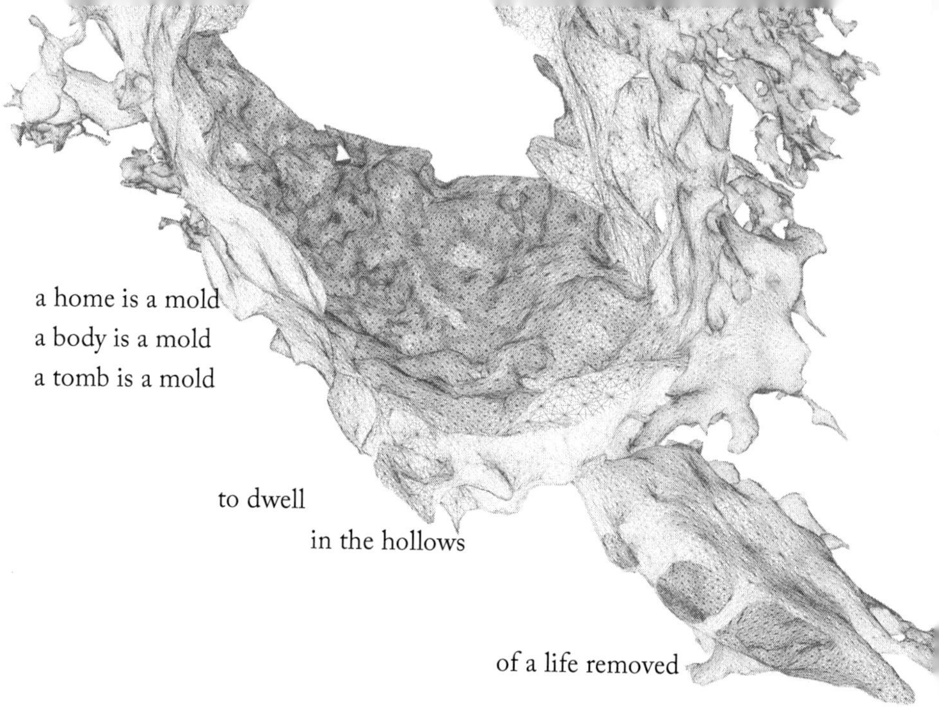

a home is a mold
a body is a mold
a tomb is a mold

to dwell
in the hollows

of a life removed

WHAT THE TUMOR SAID

When we made those sculptures of tumors

The artist said,
"Representation is only necessary in the absence of presence."

The anthropologist said,
"Every technology of revelation is embedded in protocols of occultation that regulate what is appropriate to see, what is real to see, who may see it, who may not."

The surgical oncologist in the bow tie kept whispering,
"These tumors are telling us something, they're trying to tell us something."

The parents said,
"It's that you didn't have any children to suckle."

The Lakota healer said,
"I stared into this tumor
I saw a winged one
flying in silence with the Great Being beside it:
when we take flight
we're never alone."

The analytic philosopher said,
"The image of a tumor is not a tumor."
But he and his wife stayed away from the sculptures anyway
as though they were contagious.
"It's not superstition," he said. "It's that they make you sad."

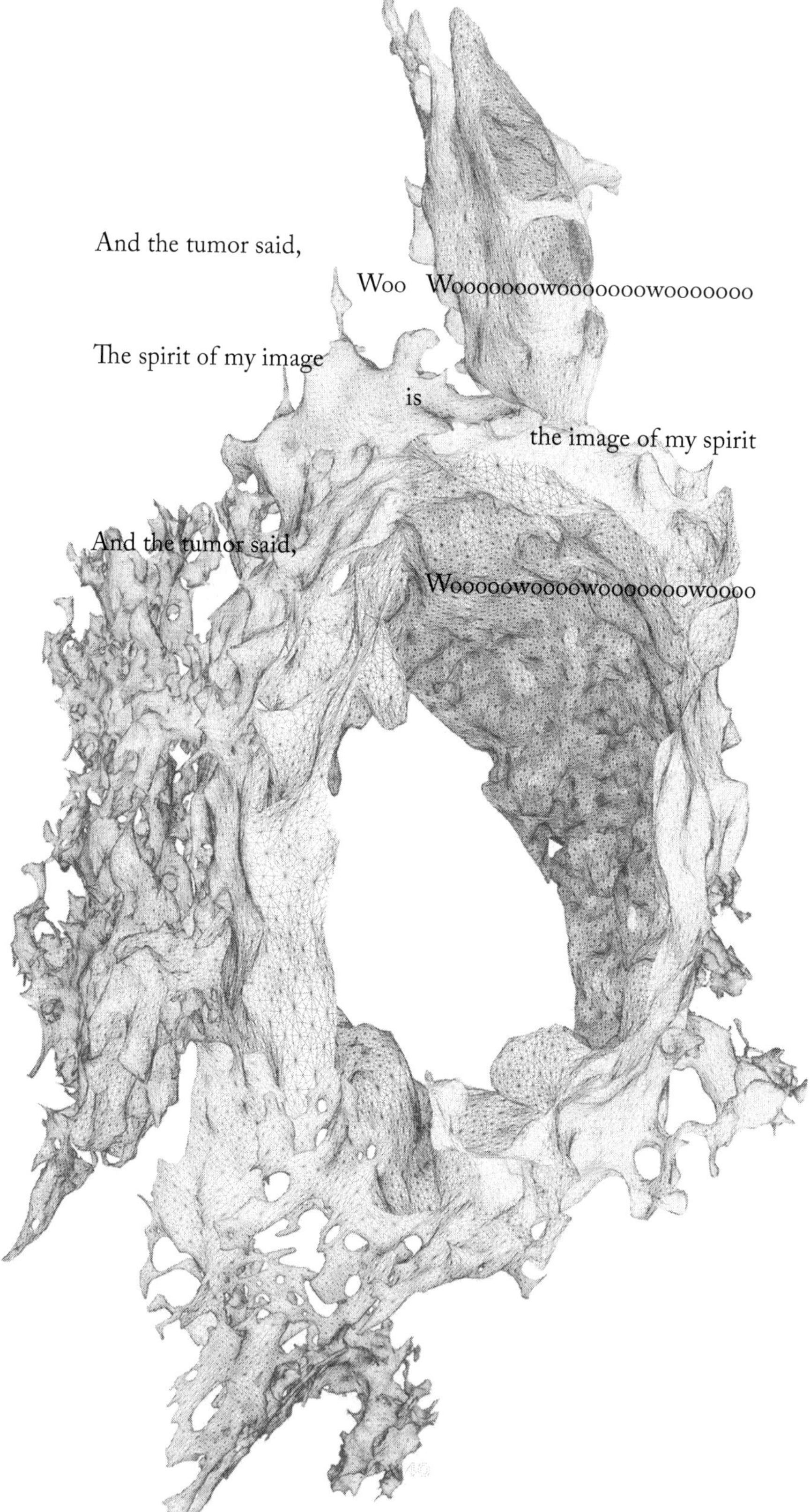

And the tumor said,

Woo Wooooooowooooooowooooooo

The spirit of my image

is

the image of my spirit

And the tumor said,

Wooooowoooowooooooowoooo

DISAPPEARING

1.40 a. m .

January 24

2015

Their appearance
makes particles unstable
and when they become unstable
they decay
when they decay
we decay
you decay
she decayed
I decayed

the rate of decay is relational

DECAY

because biology is not just biology

because life is not all life

because half-life

because radiation

because neutrinos

because alpha beta gamma

because transmutation because thought

because when you appear[xxvii]
you become 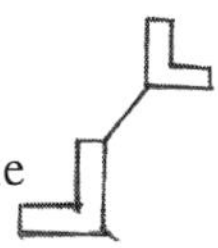

as you have been

some other

thing

ABSENCE

Leonor Caraballo 9/26/2014 12:34:18 AM :
You awake?

Leonor Caraballo 9/26/2014 12:34:30 AM :
Hola baby

Leonor Caraballo 9/26/2014 12:34:34 AM :
Vomitivo

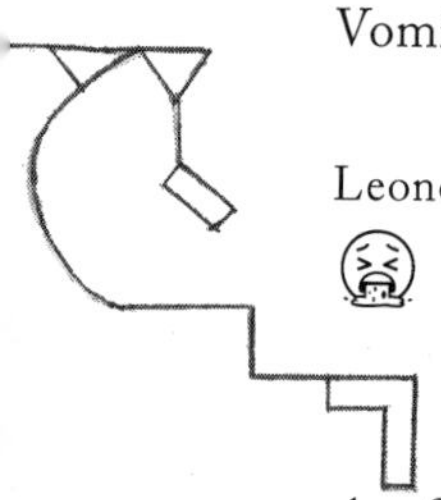

Leonor Caraballo 9/26/2014 12:34:52 AM :
🤮

aboufarman 9/26/2014 11:36:13 AM :
chu you there?

aboufarman 9/26/2014 11:44:35 AM :
bad connection let's try again?

Leonor Caraballo 9/27/2014 9:03:14 AM :
Chupie guarani

Leonor Caraballo 9/27/2014 9:03:25 AM :
How's it going?

Leonor Caraballo 9/27/2014 9:05:11 AM :
😪

aboufarman 9/27/2014 9:27:40 AM :
went fine - you seem to be in a good mood

aboufarman 9/27/2014 11:10:41 AM :
u there?

CUT

A friend, now "cancer-free," [xxviii] tells us we are crazy.

You should be resting in a peaceful environment, eating well, taking care of your body. The opposite of making a film in the Amazon. [xxxvi]

You say, "Well, what am I going to do? Sit here and wait? For a few months more of . . . ?"

Cut

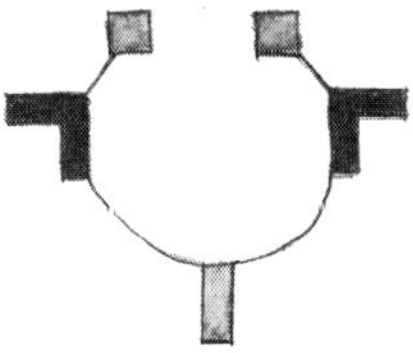

an experiment in dying

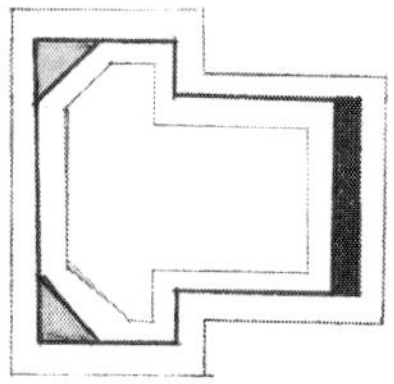

an experiment in the afterlife

everything unfolding between

Silencio!

and

Cut!

All the great forces are invisible.

Under the supermoon in the rainforest
the actress crawls inside a mosquito net

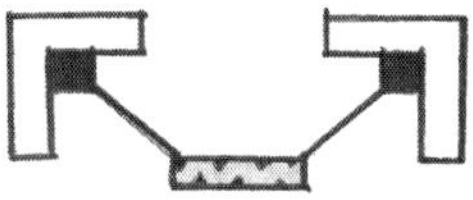

cone of light
swirl of smoke
evanescent tomorrows

mapacho icaro irake

this is you this is not you
this is an actress
an actress is a body that is both real and imagined
hers but on loan to the character
concrete and conjured,
the actress' but also the director's
hers but Leo's
not life's not death's
a corpse and an image   a corpse and a person

in the jungle   it's like in the movies
your eyes
see things where there is nothing to see
the Chullachaki appears
as someone you know
but walking on hoofs

the horizon near thick wet duplicitous

madrecita medicina

in the darkness beyond all there is is hiss

radio waves

sky

supermoon

swirl

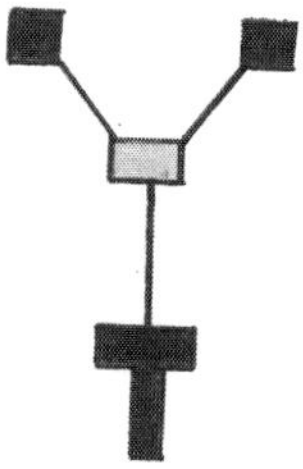

Cut!

On every surface life[xxx]
declares itself

listen—you said—

listen to...
(40,000 plant species / 16,000 tree species / 427 mammal / 1294 bird /
378 reptile / 427 amphibian / 3,000 fish species)

listen to
(7 million unknown uncounted unmeasured species[xxxi]
making waves making sugar)

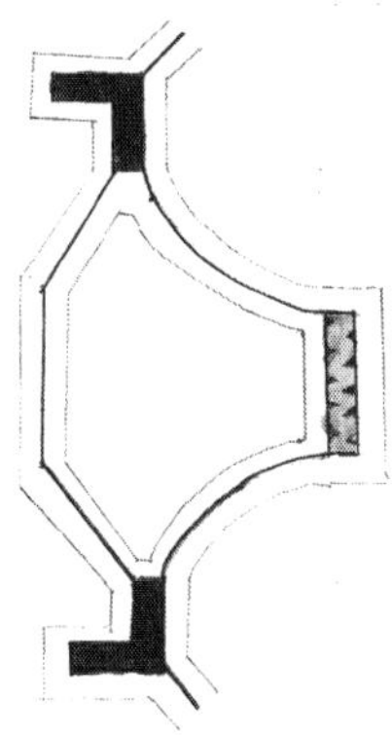

listen to this corner of the galaxy

listen to
light shoot and fold
beading the vines[xxix]
through which we dragged our visions and failings

listen to the carbon life pleats out of[xxxii]
listen to the frequencies fade

listen to life, madrecita says,
and life listens back
bats above
and pink dolphins down below [xxxiii]

once you learn to listen carefully to the night of the jungle,
the healer says,[xxxiv]
you hear the trees and vines speak up

the roots hum in their rhizomes
the Tunchi cry of all existence
from the birth pang to the death moan

for as many creatures as come to be in that jungle
exactly the same amount end up dying
—they are dying all the time, now and now and now and now and
now and . . .

Cut!

you knew

it would kill you faster

you knew

there would be no silence in the afterlife[xxxv]

you knew

you would keep on buzzing

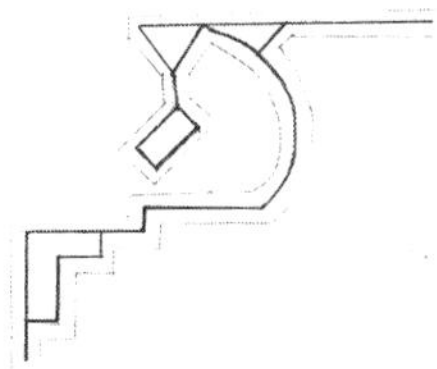

and so it did

and there isn't

and you are

Cut!

With two eyes like supermoons
you saw the film
before it ever became a film.

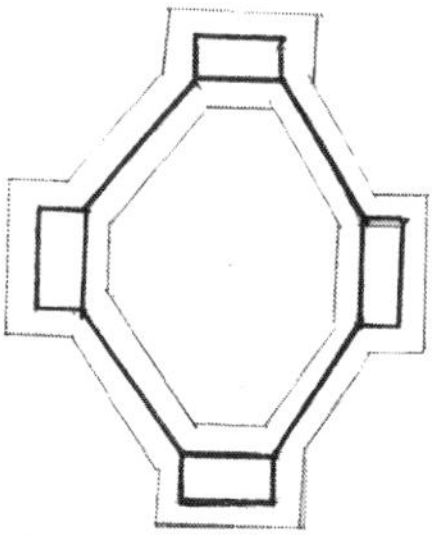

Then it became the film you never saw.

That is the hardest to live with
                    in the end

we couldn't cry when it got done
you couldn't cut your hair for the premiere
you couldn't complain about the sound
you couldn't smoke up at festivals or laugh with Arturo and Lurdes
and Matteo when we took it back to Pucallpa
we couldn't make any new memories we couldn't
take it around
this film I go around with
with you and without you I go around with this string of images you
made I go around with every take we retook I go around with every
time you say Action I go around with that shot of the supermoon I
go around with the Chullachaki and his cow hoof I go around with
the awards it didn't get I go around with the resonance of icaros I go
around with your radio signals I go around with these hallucinations
of widowhood I go around

                                        and around

the way you always went around
in the middle of the night
and got lost to discover
new things about where you thought you were until you'd find your
way again to the residency to the maloca to the movie theater to home
to bed to dream wandering beyond the habits
seeing your way out of other cones

taking images returning images (adding something to the real)[xxxix]
because
I don't know how to do anything else—you said

eyes of fuji eyes of mamiya eyes of canon eyes of leica

that's what life was, and the after too
all the impressions left[xxxvii]

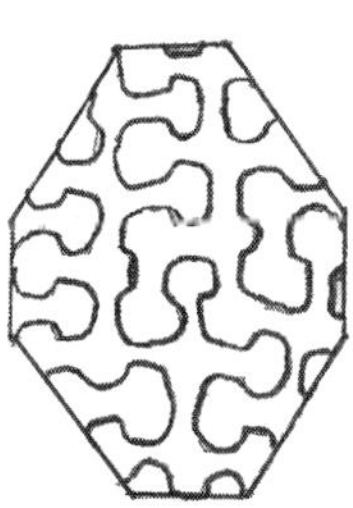

Cut!

How odd that appearance is thought
to take place in the present

when in reality   light is
a ghost[xl]

come 92 million miles carrying a trace of explosions
landing eight minutes later on your photosensitive soul[xli]
the energy of elsewhere in this afterlife we're making
without negatives or positives any prints or hard drives
this future   photonic   imagined   real

light 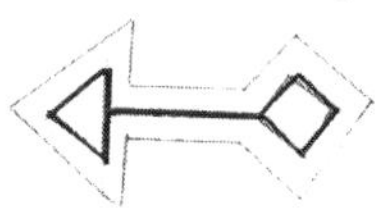

frequencies receding, images like footprints across the imagination,[xxxviii]
like someone had dropped by in the evening before you got home, a
meaning just flown off a shaking branch, the picture in the darkroom
arriving[xliii]
things here are things not quite here

every image is a ghost
as steam is of water
I of you.

IMMORTALITY

We start by not dying.

Everything is in that not.

Like when

you are born and then you don't die

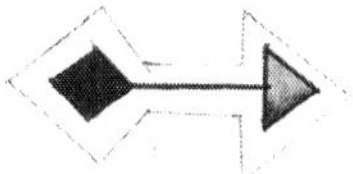

and so there you are
for the next little span of time
not dying.

Some must fight to not die
not be shot

not be

driven into the sea
not be extincted[xliv]

to survive.

To survive take another breath
get to the next moment.

Sometimes you get to the next moment whether or not
the next moment is what you want to get to
'cause maybe it's not about what you want anyway
'cause what your body wants is warmth and sugar and light
but you

you want love and creativity and glory
and regardless you just keep on not dying from moment to moment
until, before you know it, you reach that moment when   you have to.

It's hard to kick some habits
give up some fights.

I get the call
in the middle of not dying in Laughlin, Nevada.

You went, the hospital tells me,
and they decided to keep you

overnight, maybe longer.
They. Maybe. Longer.

Laughlin is a casino town named after a billionaire who wants to not die.

Well, doesn't everybody, he asks, don't you?

It's a conference on transhuman immortality. Everyone asks that question. Including the guys from Lockheed Martin

scientists, science buffs, mormons, settlers, traders, trappers
in this desert town of neon hallucinations
Whiteness stakes more claims to the future
technological-eternal

skins irradiated with a post-nuclear glow
sunlamps freon lavender-scented Lysol overly oxygenated air noble gasses deep-fry styrofoam wingless chicken pigless bacon hoofless cows tobacco petroleum pump silicon lead blood Google denial rot dripping from America's
liver[xlv]

death   cancelled

by the kaching-kaching of coins down the tin throat of slot machines run by the mafia-corporate-state complex, or by the thriving cigarette retail business the Paiute run at their downtown Tribal Smoke Shop, the largest single retailer of cigarette cancers.

What does the sand smell of in Laughlin today?

How far out is the ocean?
Can you smell it in your bones?

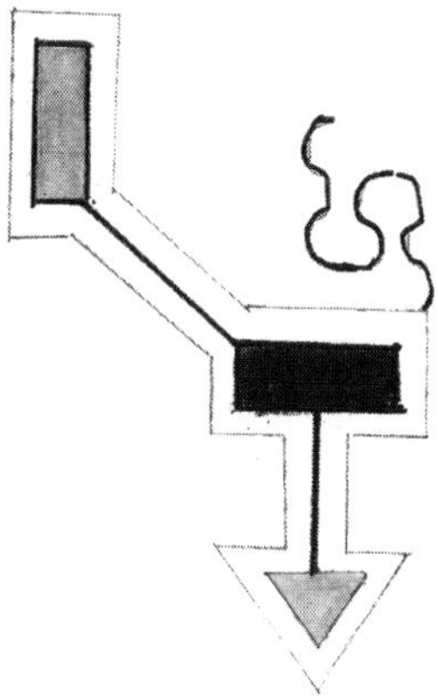

(Remember when the sphinx sat soft in stone
and your broken clavicle shone
under the full moon?
We rode mares at midnight
and the dunes undulated
with the necessity of your sea?
In that place of ascetic biology,[xlvi]
having witnessed the water recede, survived evaporation
they asked for so little those life-forms.)

On the way home, the shield of US 95

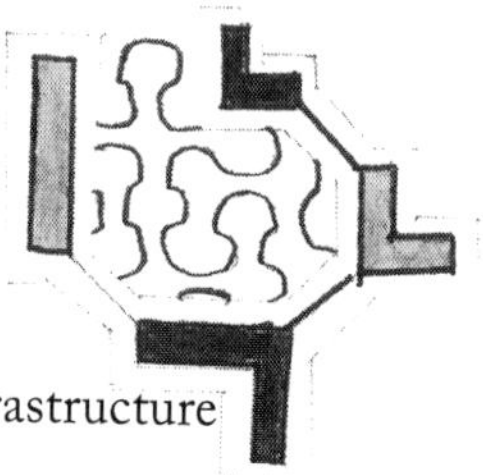

road signs

extermination into infrastructure

—paving over burials fracking over the dead

making tumors for

the living.

Numu, Nuwu, Newe.

How do I travel
this road
before me

after you

and get to call it life?

SURVIVAL

On 2014-10-31, 2014 8:14 AM, wrote:

> So, are things up and down in the platelets department ...?

On 2014-10-31, at 9:51 PM, A Farman wrote:

>

> it's hard again though her sense of acute pain has decreased, her cancer has spread viciously. it's in her neck and shoulders and all over her back and every time she moves she hears one of the bone lesions creaking closed her horizon, reminding her of more pain ahead, less possibility. Spent two of our remaining hours at Sloan last night, speaking to the new oncologist that took us days and a big fight to get an appointment with. And slowly as the oncologist proposed pain alleviation strategies one after another, we realized that's all she was going to do. There'd be no trials, no containment, no buying time. This was palliation, a rage-less easing into the night. After years of looking into therapies of all sorts, with practitioners of all sorts, months of new research, taking plants, drugs, medicines, radiation, machines, you name it—and there as the oncologist slides out of the room, having made her message clear, Leo turns to me with her eyes swelling and says, "And I'm trying so hard . . . to live."

>

>

>

> [xlvii]

>

>

To live one more second, one more cycle, one more time

what radical mutation is survival?

the need to

How did some gas and electromagnetic radiation
gain the desire
to last?

not die

And once they did, could it have gone differently?

Without all the betrayals
of biology?

of the violence of life

I mean why venom

why claws
why fangs
why darts
why traps
why horns
why thorns
why slings

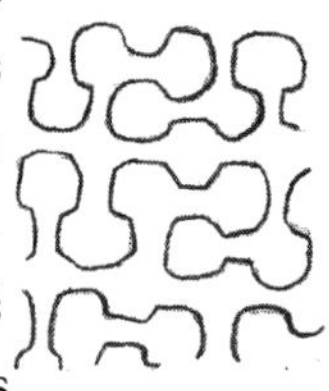

why sticks and stones and daggers and bombs and . . . ?

does the secret lie far below biology even
where the nucleus can split so beligerently?

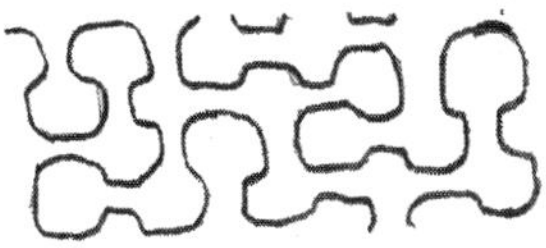

is a black hole the mother of all violence

matter expanding with the density of pain?

or is it just us
swayed so by the negative dialectic of signs?

[In Manhattan from the Sapara Amazon,
she said, white people went and found the smallest
thing in the universe
then they decided to break it in half!?]

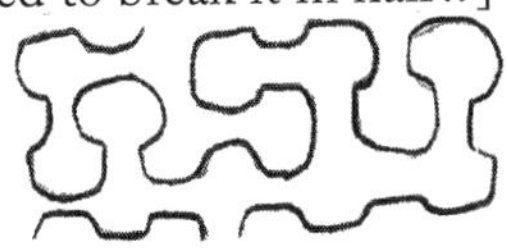

My ears to her diaphragm
the skin so taut and dry
apocalypse thumping against the chest

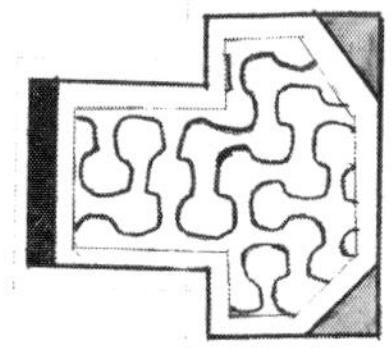

I think rib I think cage

I think
fuck the little pink teddy bear[xlviii]

I think your heart beat is no longer
a sign of life

every beat now is a beat
closer
to the end
of your heart

now

I think over 42 years
how many times has your heart beat
at 69 beats a minute?[xlix]

will mine beat a billion more

without you?

what beats are these that beat without you?

survivor's beats beating loneliness into me?

when it's still beating but we say she is dying

when we expect it to stop still

when we say she is terminal

when there is no hope
only commitment

the future is terminal

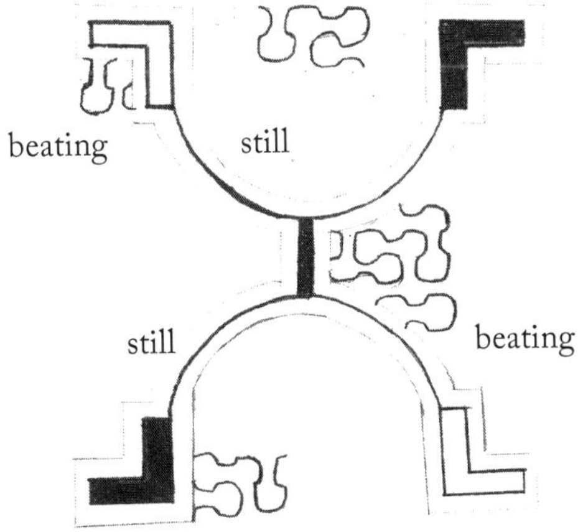

Scribbled in my notebook, a sequence of your words:

"I don't know how much time I have"
"I don't have ten years"
"I don't know how I'll be next summer"
"Take care of the film"

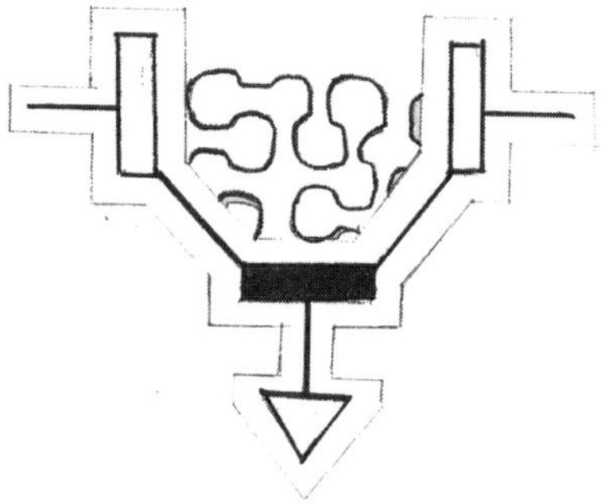

Scribbled in my notebook, a description:

"like an insect beating against the window pane"

then another note, scribbled next to it, but long after, in other ink, me going over things, trying to remember:

"was that a description of her?
or of me?"

ANESTHETIC

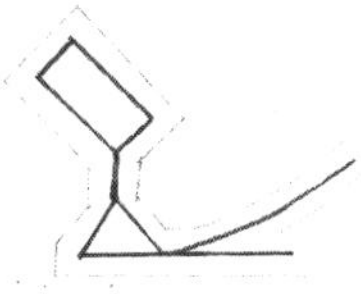

Well, now I think
I understand things
I didn't before
about survival[1]
like shoving through to get a seat
on the subway
before anyone else
because your pain was bigger.

Or was it?

The trains carry so much
pain
so many eyes call out pain

each wagon so full of pain
this city a geography of pain
so many buildings
tending to the broken
monuments of pain

everywhere broken limbs and bonds, broken lives
of pain

and every day, one hundred and thirty people die from their need to avoid excessive pain by taking too much of a substance designed to do just that

kill pain

and walking out of the hospital, all other buildings remind me that to live you need to buy to eat you need to buy to rise you need to buy to play you need to buy to learn you need to buy to relax you need to buy to dream you need to buy —
especially to dream

luxury hangs low
at the end of every synapse

on every branch, a brand

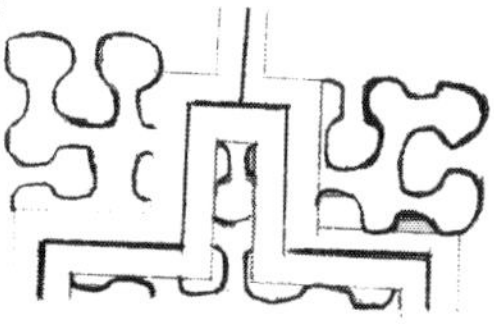

a promise in every pill every bottle of Patrón full of promises on every posturepedic better dreams inside every canoe a yacht every shack a mansion every ring a diamond every self a celebrity every mortal an immortal

the greatest production of goods made for pleasure has become inseparable from the greatest consumption of goods made to

kill pain

imagine all that is out there of Fentanyl and F-15s, Ketamine and
Kalashnikovs, Zoloft and Z-9 Blackhawk

the sheer quantity of pain killing and plain killing [lix]

ensnared is what it feels like to live

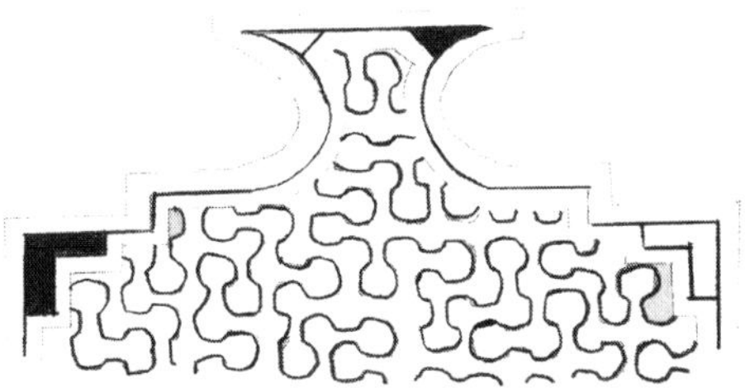

inside the pharmakon

there are pain receptors everywhere and pain centers too

but no center for suffering
neither in the brain nor in the city

and if pain is not the same as suffering
then should I understand suffering as pain plus language, pain plus
culture, pain plus interpretation, pain plus plus?

or the other way 'round, pain's what's left
when there's no interpretation
nothing appears

pain is suffering minus god
suffering minus poetry

no trembling just electricity

secular receptors shocked

secular protons
spinning
in pain
imagine that

[

imagine all the turtles

imagine them all the way down

]

General Electric, maker of MRI machines and other very sophisticated medical equipment, is also one of the world's largest military contractors. Don't you want to ask them about the relation of health machines to killing machines?[li] Ask about their stock ticker, their art collection, about progress, its relations to destruction, to hunger, to genocide?

You want to go back to the stone age? you want to die of gangrene? To drive lorries we have oil and we cure polio we treat infections and how can one even ask or question any of it, it is obvious we have it better than we used to, no one should ask or question that, of course we have it better than the past. Progress, that is what it means, the state of being convinced that this is so, that all that is behind us now, all that fear of the sabretooth and the sky when it thunders, the trouble with infections and the ulcer in the tummy, knapping flint for fire, swinging an axe to kill, clearly we have advanced, clearly, clearly. Ask them about war and its relation to survival rates,[lii] about heavy metals and mutations and superbacteria[liii] and radiation and WMD and how it all lives under one moral dome with medicine and progress.

When she was prescribed the most widely-used breast cancer drug, Tamoxifen, owned by a parent company, ICI chemicals, which is a large producer of pesticides that increase the risk of breast cancer, she asked, how do I swallow this?

You kept saying the breathing troubles
began right after 9/11.[liv]

Ours, then, is a different history
than the oncologist's
or the geneticist's.

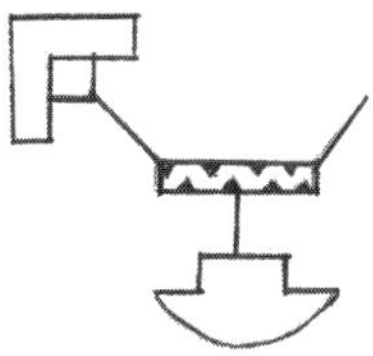

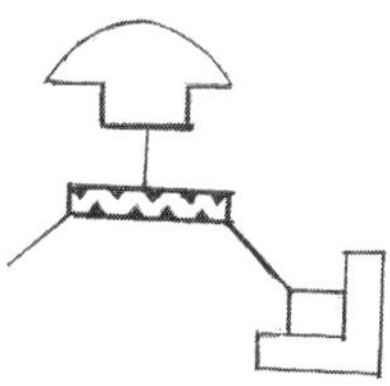

[Willkommen, bienvenue, welcome!
Fremde, etranger, stranger.
Gluklich zu sehen, je suis enchante,
happy to see you, bleibe, reste, stay.
Im Cabaret, au Cabaret, to Cabaret
the nations of the world need to continue to kill
these people, Meine Herr. No trial
just death, Meine Herr. Next!
One dead piece of Muslim garbage
millions to go.
Who wants to play Cowboys and Muslims?
Look forward to the day my grandchild will say
to me "Grandpa...whats an Arab?"
just like I asked my own
"Grandpa, whats a Sioux?"
All our bullets are virgins—never been used,
you can have 72 of them.
The real question is who let the family in in the first place?
The same morons who let in the Jamaicans,

Somalis, Sikhs and Muslims! Who else?
So...life is disappointing? Get Deported![lv]
Willkommen, bienvenue, welcome!
Fremde, etranger, stranger.
They are human animals and will be treated accordingly.[lvi]
Happy to see you, bleibe, reste, stay.
Im Cabaret, au Cabaret, to Cabaret]

WMD

toxic dust holding us in its chokehold

[fiberglass, asbestos,
jet fuel, silicon,
freon, PCBs, formaldehyde,
lead, parabens, pulverized concrete
geopolitics, General Dynamics
oil, empire
dust
to dust
topographies flattened
like Yemen like Syria like Iraq like Congo like Gaza
like the past like sand
dredged that makes concrete
that makes malls makes dreams makes towers
that fall that transmute to sandstorms
that blow us empty at the end of the world]

life and death holding us in their chokehold

[ICI chemicals,[lvii]
lindane, permethrin,
cypermethrin, captan,
capital
contradiction
carcinoma]

how do I swallow this?

[dogs bark all night
demons worm out of your pores]

In the anesthetic age,[lviii]
we found no pain medication
whose side effects wouldn't cause greater pain.

So if not the levophranol or the fentanyl patch or the lidocaine or the hydromorphone or the xeloda,
how about I move the pillow under your elbow
then under your hip your neck your shoulder?

Every night we build a fortress out of pillows,
architecture of care [lix]
ritual of pain
killing

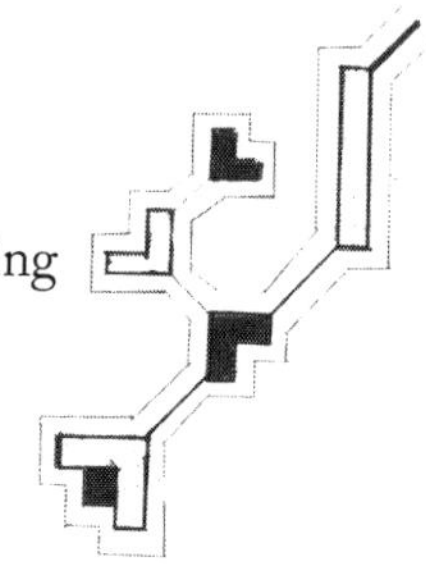

the bare bones dailiness of things when you are sick
and dying.

[The resident anesthesiologist gave you the common orientation test to see if you're there, if you had come back from the Propofol, returned to the land of language. He asked, "Do you know where you are?" You said, "Yes, Club Med."
Before he could reorient himself, you said, "I don't want to die here, I need to go home."]

Questions about anesthesia may include:
where does one go when one goes out like that?
where is that there?
are you there now?

Leo?

Do they want you to wake up?
Wake, waking, awakened, woke, awakening, reveal yourself,
open your eyes, stand up, rise up, appear, raise your fist.

Questions about anesthesia may include:
whence do you reckon we make our appearance
in the world?

And
where you been?

We stole you home.

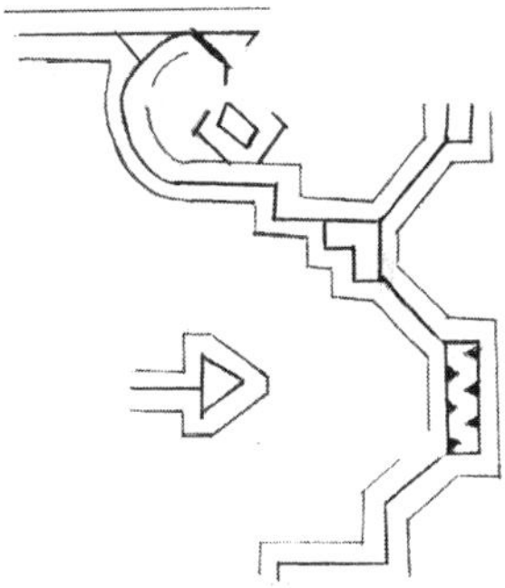

SHIT

What laxative should I take? Kazuko's pills with
the Cleansemore? Or Swisskriss?
Swisskriss is a laxative?
Isn't it?
Maybe we should change, because these things are addictive,
you know?
Senna is addictive?
Once you're on it, you can't shit without it, so we alternate?
Yes so maybe the Swisskriss.
Do you feel constipated?
I shat diahrrea earlier so . . .
But now?
I don't know, it's the chemo maybe makes me more diarrhetic.

Do you want some apples? I boiled apples earlier you can eat soft apples.

Yes.

That's good, your appetite's back.

Then you sleep then you throw up then you say,
"It's the sleep apnea mask
or maybe the chemo pills
or maybe the probiotic gels,
that oxygen gun Matteo gave me made me puke too."

When we go for a little stroll outside to get fresh air you say, "Maybe oxygen makes me nauseous."

maybe oxygen[lx]

maybe life

life   in the maybe

this may be life

the maybe life

In the era Before Cancer you used to say, "I hate this life."

as though if you had appeared in another life you might have liked
it much more that life but in this one people said one thing and did
another they didn't pay attention to detail they were careless men
were all show and tell they watched porn were partial to shaved
armpits pussies blow-up dolls blow-up muscles fancy cars they hit
their daughters pathetic women listened shaved pussies didn't hit back
got sick you wanted to hit back you did hit back you wanted a world
where you didn't have to hit back people hypocrites even me cowardly
traitor smiling sycophant always wanting to be loved while you took
the trouble to be disliked took it head on seeing trouble differently as
we saw different things as trouble we saw life as different things we
saw we as though we saw we as we as we
as we

Mistletoe injection? Ganja oils? Oxycodone
and Duexis, alternating?
What's that one, Trazadone?
I'll just take the Nyquil.
You read out the label, "Made in Israel."

I say, I'm not sure it's time for boycott, peel off the label.
You say, I want to peel off this body.

In the era Before Cancer you always used to say,
"I want to change
my body."

And so many times you did
become more more man more woman more
beast more insect more bird
more we less we
less you

less me.

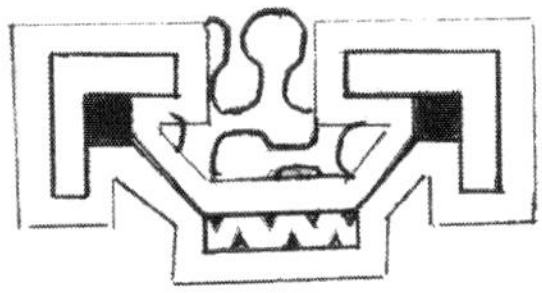

Lorazepam stabilizes the waves but even so I hold the plastic bag
up and here it comes, the night lamp making the yellow vomit glow
through the plastic just below the Keyfoods logo, and like a stupid
chatbot I ask, "How do you feel?"

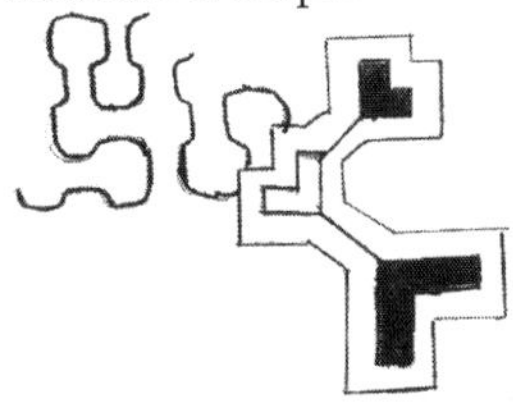

I don't want this time to end—

it's a horrific feeling for me to have while you are dying:
I'd also had it before
but when you weren't dying it wasn't a horrific feeling.

Now it's all I have:
you like this, me with this feeling.

Now there is no feeling that's not sunk
one foot in the horrific.

How much longer will it take?
I don't know what time to live by, 3 or 10? days, months or years?
And what difference does that make?

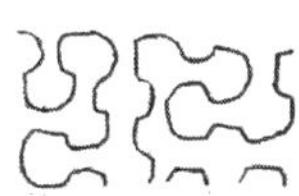

Can I sleep on the catheter side?

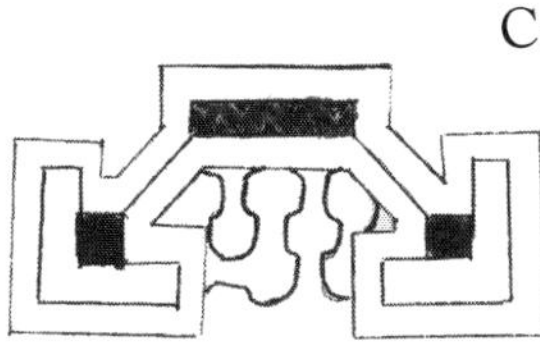

What units, what grammar, what feel for time left?

Biology is time   time is money
and oncology manages the relationship—
slice up and distribute time in the holding pen.

You ask, Will you remember my face?

Have you noticed how smell and nausea are related in a way
that touch and nausea aren't?
I hate my smell.
What smell?
Urine and blood.
I can only smell it when I kiss your thighs and play
with your pubic hair.
Will we be able to sleep tonight?
I don't know.
Over the years it's been through bodily fluids that we got to more love.
I know what you mean.
We drank each others' pee.
Snot tears cum.
Blood.
Well what do you want me to bring you have to eat something you
can't eat love.
Coconut flakes or maybe I want a burger or how about a pear? What
can I eat?
Well listen to your body, what does your gut tell you?
My gut tells me I'm fucked.

Enzymedica Digest Capsules Blood Builder Capsules Enzymedica PH-Basic-Capsules Melatonin Tablets iFlora Multi-Probiotic-Capsules Diphenhydramine HCI Artecin Capsules Ultimate Enzymes Capsules Sx-Fraction-Maitake Mushroom Tablets 365 B-Complex-With Folic Acid Tablets Marrow Plus-Ji Xue Teng Tablets Acidophilus Plus FOS Capsules Innate-Coenzyme B Complex Capsules Betulinic Acid Concentrate Giant Redwood Young Shoots Sequoia Gigantea Young Shoots Bilberry Young Shoots Sweet Chestnut Buds Black Poplar Buds Sinus Eliminato Lemon Tree Bark Citrus Limonum Holly Young Shoots Exemestane Tablets ABT-888 Capsules Grape Vine Buds Juniper Young Shoots Rosemary Young Shoots Black Elder Buds Dog Rose Young Shoots SYS Nigelia Oriental Plane Tree Buds Trazodone HCL Tablets Gaia Cat's Claw Bark Rhizome and Root Valerian Nervous System PSC Caraway Rootlets Mountain Pine Buds Californian Poppy Buds Dandelion Embryonic Roots Fig Buds Head Arresto Hornbeam Buds Black Currant Buds Bramble Young Shoots Caraway Rootlets Mistletoe Young Shoots Syspassiflora Integratore Alimentare Ecologically Wildcrafted Chuchu Huasi Burdock Root Beta I 3D Glucan Stool Softener Liver Cleanse St. John's Wort Oil Kava Kava Root Arresto Prevento Nervous System Calming Passion Flower Dexamethasone Elixir Olivier Jeunes Pousses Olea Europaea Broncho Modulato Dry Mouth Oral Rinse Oxycodone Solution Buis-Jeunes Pousses Buxus Sempervirens DLPA Caps Extra Strength Lung Decongestant Eucalyptus Chest Rub Enhanced Super Digestive Enzymes Herbal Laxative Tabs Ensomeprazole Magnesium Marvlix Ondansetron Oxycodone Complejo Antioxidante Dissolved Oxygen Trace Minerals, Plant Source Amino Acids, and Enzymes Alkaline Booster with Antioxidant Valerian Root Ibuprofen and Famotidine Cleanse More Dextromethorphan HBR Raw Probiotics Multi-Probiotic

Dietary Supplement Capsules Oxycodone HCL Zolpidem Tablets
Pantoprazole Tablets Dexamethasone Tablets Diazepam Tablets
Lorazepam Tablets Natural Sleep Aid Pasteurized Saline Laxative
CBD Hemp Oil Motrin PM Aspirin Tablets Acetaminophen Caplets
Ibuprofen ABT-888 Oil Aromatherapy Aurum Mercury Corrosiu
Ganja Oil Natural Healing Aid Antica Tanuta Giovanna CBD
Hempoil Olopatadine Hydrochloride Ophthalmic Solution Baby
Powder Pure Alkaloid Suspension Oil Medical Cannabis Aloe Gel
Mercurius Corrosiuo Miralax Aceite Oleo Algesic Salve Nucynta
Tablets Hydromorphone HCL Tablets Tramadol APAP Tablets
Morphine Tablets Capecitabine Tablets Levorphanol Tablets Valium
Colace Triamcinolone Acetonide Copaifera Paupera Lubricant
Eye Ointment Apfelbaummistel Praparat Alcohol Prep Maytenus
Macrocarpa B-5 Panthotenic Acid Amazonian Bark Vicks Dayquil
Severe Tilo Passifora Valeriana Claritin-D Herbatonin Tylenol Sinus
Dulcolax Bisacodyl Glycerin Suppository Malehgu Bark Tenre Para
El Higado Zeolite Tea Pollen

crush and mix together in blender, pour into sealed
container, label, store in a cool place for the day of mabada

when you are ready to become her

LAST QUESTION

When you saw the pregnant woman on the street and said,
"A proposition for a new life."

—we start out as an idea
—conception is preconception

—exit the birth canal and take on flesh
—flesh fills with ideas and language and codes and norms—
becomes more than flesh—

—until death[lxi] again renders us but flesh—

emptied
of all that had overinflated us with all this being—

Two eternal absences:
in the prior you are no one: in the posterior you were someone: and what happens in between must be the strangest thing in the universe.

Do you remember, Lilly,
her last words when she waved us over
and held our hands
on either side of her death bed
and she, who was never
much into talk, said,
"Let's talk . . . "
and then said
nothing more after that
ever

but held on to our hands anyway?

will you let me go, life?

will you let me go, death?

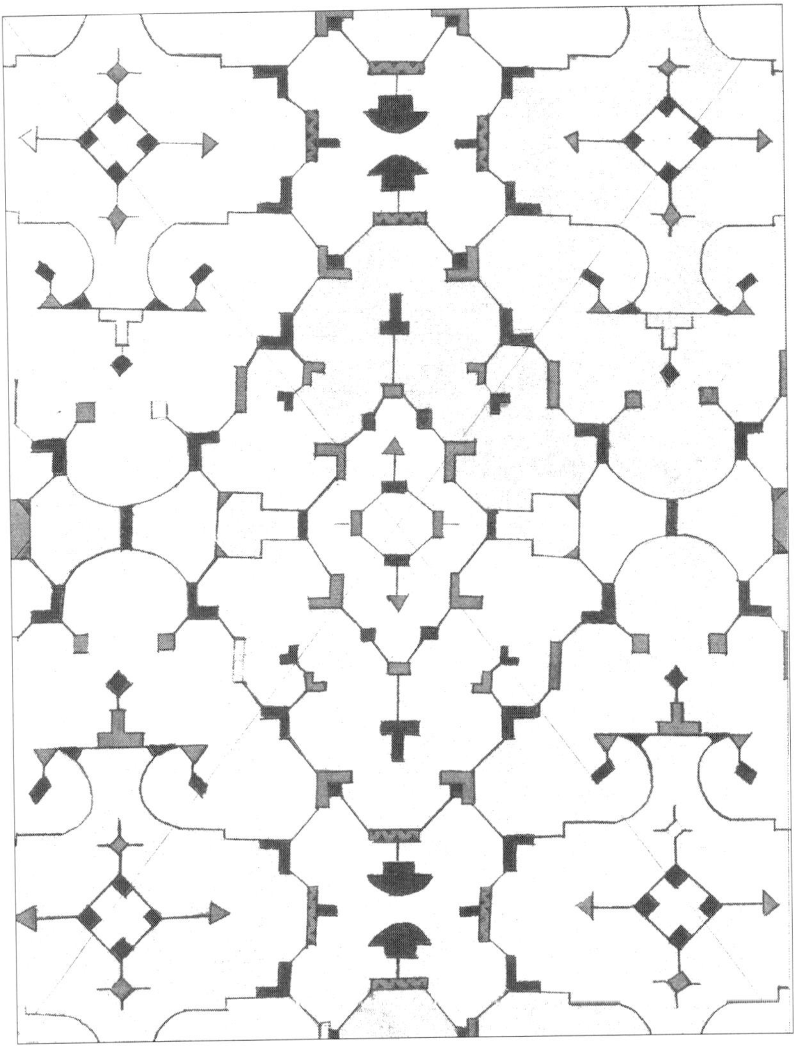

REAPPEARING

The wind comes from there.
The grass comes from there.
The bugs come from there.
Water comes from there.
Life comes from there.
Ghosts come from there.

NO SILENCE

The night sky broke open with snow and in the morning I washed the body I washed between the toes traced the clavicle ran a rivulet across the forehead behind the ears wiped the dribbles around the mouth, the lips tight and tighter the nostrils, I put a finger against the bunion on the left against the bunion on the right water ran off the arms off the fingers bony still, off the wrist twisted still, I flushed the navel laid a hand on the vagina palming the belly, the belly bloated, and so bloated the thighs, soft the skin, like youth, but taut like death, stretched like a drum around the scars so many scars so many cuts from so many tubes so many blood draws incisions insertions ideas for improvement and now the veins shrunk more even   dry   drying dried   and I want to put the hose in there and fill them again with fresh currents and flows, before it is lowered below the skin of the earth waiting for her moonlight, the new food of ancient creatures below the snowcrust ready to welcome her body to squirm through the parts I touched last, touch them differently take them in and break them down differently grind her parts with stones in their gizzard metabolise her flesh micro-organize her soft tissue spin her protons transform her into what she even she could not have imagined for she surely became other things so many many things but who has the count of what all she did become?

What all she had been?

Studies show that widowers die faster.

Attributed to compromised immune systems, endocrines, autonomous nervous system breakdowns, forfeiture of reason, dementia, blocked neurotransmitters though it all just means

loss

of resonance, of what spun your protons,[lxii] folded your proteins, the meanings that connected ur synapses, lifted your orgasm, painted a future common to two people moving into it together, one tuned to the other, microbiomes in symbiosis, a commons, circadian rhythms coordinated, expectant, matching the rotations of planets at one end and the rotations of The Other at the other

and when The Other's gone
the ensuing molecular confusion we call

loss

me in the mirror seeing a hole in me we call loss
the imprint of your back on the mattress we call loss
            you there not there
maybe there   maybe

they misarranged the universe today
and we call it loss

ontological discombobulation
            you can die from it
from not finding things where they are supposed to be
from finding holes where others are meant to be
            you can die
you can want to
you can
swim out in to the middle of the ocean because you said to yourself if I
swim far enough where I won't be able to swim back home then I can
be gone forever let the hole take me the water there are no solidities
go get immersed forever
but you don't
the light bends you at the horizon
that selfsame body calls you back
home to look at the bottle of morphine and think how much of this
do I need to get back to the middle of that ocean?

What keeps keeping us here?

ORPHIC

Is there in all of human history
a bigger idiot?

One simple rule to stick to and what did he do?[lxiii]

Chorus:
"What about 'don't turn around'
did you not understand?"

He could have ended up back on the surface with her
brought someone back from the dead
just anyone would have been a feat
but she was his great love and what did he do!

Chorus:
"What about 'don't turn around'
did you not understand?"

Imagine Eurydice at that moment when
trailing behind him, their hands clutched hard,
a crack of light from the surface about to cut
through the darkness...

Chorus:
"What about 'don't turn around'
did you not understand?"

When she saw his head
begin to turn...
that moment...
and every one after that...

Chorus:
"We'll have to get used to this now."

Orpheus feels regret and invents lyrical music
and becomes the sad, creative genius, his lyre strings vibrating with the sublime frequencies of the tragic.

But what about Eurydice
condemned to boredom
repeating that moment in her head forevermore
wishing Orpheus had broken his neck?

Chorus:
"We'll have to get used to this now."

And what about Eurydice eyeing Persephone from a dark quiet corner, thinking with resentment, "At least she gets to go up half the time and the other half she's the wife of the king of hell. I have to sit around in darkness and shake my head all day because that foolish boy Orpheus couldn't, just once in his life, follow instructions?"

They, in a world without music
condemned to parse the distinction between error and betrayal.

Chorus:
"What about 'don't turn around'
did you not understand?"

Maybe, eventually, she thought, living with him forevermore
would have been too much a punishment, fuck Orpheus.

Chorus:
"We'll have to get used to this now.
We'll have to get used to this now."

MISCELLANEOUS WONDER

how close it has been this death
always, suddenly

how dear
how speechless it leaves us in the demand to say
something

isn't that what we do for the dead, say something?

the spiders crawling across our pages
are gone now
leaving webs, hanging threads, traces in the air
suspended as memories

the grass long still in the pampas, horses, and a camera,
a hoofstorm of love, the sweat foaming on the rumps

how far this death,
the horizon another shade, the angle of the clearing acute beyond
those two Ombus

then you just rode off—and when i asked why,
you made it more undecipherable, even if i know now you went to
embrace a pure orange sunset.
There you shrugged, "So what?   Lick my corpse."

I take with me at least the shape of the movement of your spiderhand as it was tracing life on a day in October two years earlier in a maloca in the Amazon

:

breathing def helps remind me that I'm still alive

.

what do I read when I read your journal? what do I see when I see your hand on the page, when I touch it? What do I touch when I touch the page you had touched with yours, what did you shed on that page of your skin, of your dandruff, your mutations, your hydrogen protons, your pain the shape of your mouth, your tongue, your uterus in a bucket in a maloca in the Amazon what do I read when I read

:

The pain never ceased there were short sporadic moments of great bliss and vibrations connected to the icaros the voice of Arturo is in several places at the same time sometimes I saw patterns but mostly the trip was about my pain how to breathe into it the alter-ego was there a voice that instructed me to thank to be thankful be grateful for the food and water sometimes it was hard to listen to these lessons had to keep changing position because my back was so uncomfortable the breathing became smooth and long but occasionally I choked myself choked hay mucho mas adelante mas cosas que descrubrir

.

I am surprised by the geography of death

to my right the seven seas

to my left the mineshafts of the cerebrum

When I wake I ask the psychologists
and other assembled mind readers
"what was that down there?

What depths did I plumb?
Whom did I encounter?
What was it I heard?
Can you tell me?"

I search for the voice
small smoky
squeaking out of a matchbox
and wonder if dreams
now are the only land
where we can come to meet
on equal footing, you and I?

you know her like the tree knows the wind

it is moved

you bastard hijo de puta you took over our bed
you fuck people in it
you let them use the bathroom
you're wearing my jewelry
you took over the house it's always full
all these people coming through
you show off the art the kitchen show off your love how nice you are
the living are overexcited, yakettiyaking
about their preferences tastes
desires endangering the pottery the peace
the paint is peeling the wall is stained the closet is a mess the window
leaks the souls are disturbed
I can't staaaand it you never could take care of things
and also don't keep all my stuff throw 'em out
don't you remember I threw everything out
my art too
all this shit and you think you are honoring me?

to know her is to notice
the rustle in you as she passes through

then says goodbye

you know, fuck you too, you know how it feels to be your proxy
to be your survivor to make a film with you I knew would kill you
to have to give you the last drops of morphine so the hospice nurse
could pronounce death, to work with your lovers, to live
with your strength above me your eye behind me your lens before me
your obsessive compulsive discernment framing every fucking thing
just right you don't know what it feels like every fucking day to make
art to make decisions to write without you here your widower your
zombie

I thought you are saying I am here?

You are, but you know what I mean!

When you go see a spirit medium
people ask you if you believe
and I wonder what you have to believe
in order to go see a therapist
and why people don't ask you that?

The mail keeps invoking her
the bureaucracies and catalogs
and loan sharks want her alive too.

LEAKY

those who live with the dead

move with the dead
walk with the dead
carry the dead
fit the dead
into a canoe
on the Amazon
holding the sunbrella
for shade

our liquidities and equanimities

our bodies leaky distal
linked to death by thinking death drinking death smelling death
tasting death seeing death touching death seeping
death

a body oozing on the margins
vulnerable to influence
to entry, to magnetism, to alternating currents, flows, lightning, plants,
air, cloud, fire, love, storm,
dependency, vulnerability, irrationality, suggestibility,
its crumbled future pouring down an hourglass

a body exempted from reason excites
and disturbs in equal measure
they want to banish me or fuck me
or look at me with so much deep understanding and say, “It must be hard. Time will help.”

fuck time
araq will help

the great civilization curates its corpses in cabinets
I sniff inside your kangaroo boots

your mascara brushes my lashes
your hat has some hair   in it   some DNA
the sheets
the rings too
everywhere your fingerprint
on me   impressed   my form   inhabited
my mind   a mold for ghosts

OTHERS DREAM

email-dream 1[xlii]

>

dear abou
she came in to my dream just now during my afternoon nap - she had beautiful bangs that got brushed from one side to another - we were hanging out she was well, but i didnt want to bring up the fact that she is dead so i hugged her and she gently protested and I explained that i dont get to hug her enough i was so happy to be with her – and you have you been remembering any of your dreams? with her?

sending you hugs

e-dream 2

>

I dreamt of Leo last night. It was crystal clear and real. She was lithe and beautiful and sitting on a chair, with a bunch of her clothes on a bed. When I saw her I immediately began crying. She laughed (a sort of "ai you!"), but it was kind and full of love, and for a moment she was pained to see my sorrow.

And then we took off. And the room turned into a corridor that turned into an entrance to a huge theater, full of people. Hundreds of them. Essentially every single person in the theater (hundreds of them), began writing on small pieces of material (muslin? silk?), they began writing down their memories of Leo.

Until soon

e-dream 3

>

we were walking around the space of the maloca in the day time. she was in a good mood. she said she did not have any more pain where she was now and was getting close to the spirit of the red radish. she was also suggesting to extend the best shots of the cut.

Thinking of you

e-dream 4

>

she was just in my dream right now during my half a day nap. we were hanging out. she was well, but i didnt want to bring up the fact that she is dead. i hugged her and she gently protested. I explained that i dont get to hug her enough. she had beautiful bangs that got brushed from one side to another. i was so happy to be with her.

Sending love

e-dream 5

>

Was in a Greek-Indian temple with white marble floors and Indian dancers spinning around me. I closed my eyes and had beauitful visions of light. When I openned them, and looked on the ground, I saw Leonor's name etched onto the marble

:)

e-dream 6

>

Leo's been in my dreams a lot. Last night too. She's always busy at work and I'm usually hesitant to disturb her.

Love

e-dream 7

>

It was with Leo and you. We got to a gallery that stretched out, and below us were the rolling hills. The gallery was covered by some sort of "roof", but what was amazing was that there were trees growing upside down from the roof, so imagine you look up at trees that stretch down to you. The trees were tinged with the most beautiful cobalt blue.
You said: Leo and I have been working on this since last year. See how the trees have grown?
Besos

e-dream 8

>

We were making another film or maybe the same film but then the floor was burning, the tripod was burning, our feet burning – and we were saying, "Let's keep going"

e-dream 9

>

it's hard to explain. perhaps they were just dreams. but she talked to me. she talked to my moral. to straight me up. not very different from when she was alive.

e-dream 10

>

Hello Abou ,,you know my name is xxxxx and i used to be a close friend of leonor years ago when she was living in argentina ,,,i owe her all the persian music she shared with me ,,a great treasure i still listen very often ,,,, when she left this world i dreamt with her twice or three times ,,a very vivid dream i dont use to have very often and im dreamt that she was saying goodbye to me with her big smile ,,,saying me something like `èvery thing is fine ´´she was in a good mood ,,,then i had another dream and she have a hug in that dream ,,and i was sad in the dream ,,i was crying because she was saying goodbye again ,,,,it was very shocking ,,i dont have any particular believe in after life ,,,,but these dreams were so vivid ,,very clear her presence ,,very shocking ,,,i dont know perhaps was my unconcius because i felt very shocked and affected by that time for her disappearence ,,,,

my regards

>>>>>>>>>>>>>>>>>>>>>>

CRY

Why do I cry? [lxiv]

Why do I cry in the morning?

Why do I cry at midnight?

Why do I cry when trucks go by?

Why do I cry into my cereal? into my quinoa? why do I cry in my chest? in my head? in my elbows and toes? into the toilet bowl, the ceramic sides so cold on my palms? why do I cry alone? why do I cry in corpse pose? at the end of every class? why do I cry in museums? in hypnosis? in church pews? in the maloca? in front of Think Coffee? in the back of Think Coffee? the movie theater? why do I cry with my head against that doorframe? when my fingertips remember the line of hair below your belly button? when I walk? when I sit near the mulberry trees? near the river? why did I cry on the A train when it got delayed? in seat 30L on LATAM 531 to Lima? why did I cry when I turn on your iphone? and find the last photo? of you? in bed, directing remotely the last shot ever shot of the last film you ever filmed?

Grief rose out of the ocean
and returned dropping from the sky

it's where we start
infants crying
for that world of water we lost
5 billion years ago and keep in us

the ocean amniotic, saline, snot, spit, semen, sweat, saliva of time, the human effluvium the flow we know as life and loss

ejected from the world of water, alien
landed in the world of oxygen, alien
come from the comforts of darkness, alien

Creature of the crust, I cry to survive

I cry proteins, protons, ions, mucin, glucose, lipids, enzymes, dirt sometimes, sometimes sand

in my eyes
in each tear many pains
other pasts, crumbled
other loss coursing through us
each tear dropping so many other sorrows

from the other inseparate to the other separate I cry

I cry and taste the other

the being of water I am not
the sky of light I am not
the past I am not
the dead I am not
I cry your presence
your condensations curl on my lip
waters of the watery planet[lxvi]   drip
waters of your driest eyes   drip

our bodies are composed 70% of grief
I cry
and know my dead
are of mist, fog, evaporate, steam, ghosts of water moving between
states[lxv]
without whom there is no cycle
          of love, the wet portal between others
other realms, heres and theres, theirs and mine, you, me, visibles,
invisibles, I hear you, how are you today? I feel you, how are you today?

This is not happening
in my head

it goes on in the guts

in the soil in the clouds
in the marrow of time

maybe in your head too

grief in the crust in the mantle in the lithosphere

its inner core the lungs of lava
its open node the throat of sadness open open open

open the window of a car moving 70 miles an hour
open the mouth wide and scream into the open
other drivers staring
from behind their closed panes

to scream into the holes in the world

is to know screaming
is a kind of language not the language of pain
but the language of bearing pain

is to know the afterlife is loud, like love, surrounded
by wails

the lament the dirge the keen
what mourning song is without a scream?

tears come from the tear duct
but the crying comes from elsewhere

that horizon of orange, that sky of ashes,
that forest of fires, that frequency of foam,
that nebula, that luna of sleep,
that field of disappearance

weep and on the other side things will not be the same

LATAM 2649 rips through the clouds
I land and Leo appears,
          she asks where her poems are.

I say, you threw them into the sea
          you liked the sea remember
          you wanted to be in it and take me with you
          shift the salt content.
You say nothing
          you stare.

When the dead stare at you
          you must cry, then scream
          a little, not from fear
          but because there is nothing else to do.

Are you still here? Where is the flotation device
                              and the breathing apparatus?

You say, come back to bed.
I say, one more glass.

Love is negotiation.

I am still not sure how the singularity of your death
connects up to all the other deaths
          but it does
          and where that happens, it opens up
                    a possibility we call justice.
Bring me home, I say.
You say nothing.

MOURN

Hospice hands out its brochure of platitudes in the last days saying,
talk to each other make peace put things in order apologize celebrate
listen touch say I love you I forgive you I will be ok you will be ok
thank you for the art we made I know it was difficult sometimes
working with me with me too yes with you too I was so moody you
would scream sometimes and you you would break things yes I would
and blame you for not knowing the software I would blame you too
for being sloppy I am sloppy but I am happy we were together me too
we made good work mostly yes together we made good work I don't
regret any of that no we couldn't leave each other sometimes you hated
me sometimes you wanted to kill me you wanted to leave sometimes
I did you too but there was something always stopped it my cancer
that too but love yes something we didn't always get it maybe in the
future we would have broken up maybe now we don't have to please
don't cry now if you cry I will lose it I won't I will make sure I'll take
care of you after I die I will take care of you after you die too make
sure Amir sees the film and Michael too I will I have a list it would be
nice to have a healing center here yes I know you had such a good idea
all the different modalities I have good ideas sometimes I will do that
somehow assemble a home for healing

but it can never be enough
the problem overspills
          the bounds   of all you can possibly say
because
the real problem is not what you haven't said but all what you can't say
ever again after that

— and maybe all what you can

anyway, maybe
it's how you keep on talking
to them—like this?—

        and no
        no hospice will teach you that
                no therapist no counsellor

elders in other zip codes can guide you:
to ensure a potent afterlife
mourn strong   protest the living   call in the dead

[Recommended measures include pulling out hair, hearing voices, talking, asking apparitions who they are, dressing up, getting possessed, rubbing red ochre on your chest, chicken shit, pigeon blood, midstream piss, piercing epidermal barriers, blocking mirrors, polishing mirrors, erecting altars, taking mushrooms, dancing the resurrection, butoh, protesting, fighting the police, fainting, falling, throwing up, throwing out, trying everything.]

        you are this hair, this necklace this ring this skirt I wear, this pillbox, this camera, this keyboard, this image, this tumor, this morphine I keep in the fridge its time still to pour, I taste you how are you today?

                                how are you not?

Do not fear the soft orange glow

soft

closure would require that I kill you for good

or myself

orange

mourning is how I keep you alive in me still

and keep me alive too

glow

do not fear the soft orange glow of human beings
when they are not there

I see you erupting
out of your grave
in grass and dandelion and caterpillar in milkweed and beetle and
mite
and I know the water in us is the water of the earth
the water in us is the water of the sky[lxvi]
the atmosphere holds the grief over our heads
releases it in tempests
cumulonimbus swirling with protons charged
electric liquid grief

sit up, listen

that is what a storm does
we hug our knees and listen to the sky hit up against the window
panes, a future
                    trembling and raindrop bespeckled

tear-sight is rain-sight storm-sight ghost-sight the tempest in us
striking everything you see everything you see kept alive in brine for
the dead drink from the lake fed by the tears of the bereaved[lxviii] who
later die and drink from the same lake
they had once cried into the same one being cried into now by those
mourning them and cried into by being

soul crying being

                              sky crying ocean

My notebook says:
"I lie down and cry her name and wail and I gain more energy."[lxvii]

It is only once he is cried for
that the Yoruba high chief is declared dead.[lxix]

And it was only after loud crying and recitations
that Hsuan-tang managed to make the Buddha's shadow
re-appear on the cave wall.

In Inner Mani, grieving women would seclude themselves for more
than 40 days and pull their hair and scream. [lxx]
In Inner Mani, "Silent death is the bad death."

Francis of Assissi went blind he cried so much.

When someone died in Anatolia, mourners would cut their face
mixing blood and tears, life and death.

One of the first things colonial rulers, church leaders and post-colonial secular states did was eliminate local ways of doing death, placing prohibitions on funerals and mourning rites which were felt to be both politically and epistemically dangerous: the affective power that could mobilize the colonized with an excessive zeal for freedom, and the passionate attachment to continuity that muddied the rational separations between dead and alive, object and subject, ruler and ruled.

So, then, dears

where have we left to go
to cry with others?[lxxi]
I want to cry
with people who cry
who know how to cry with others
to draw out the cry
held in others.

Who are the deathless who do not mourn?
the tearless who do not cry?[lxxii]

the inundation[lxxiii]

from which life

fire

from

which

tears

with it we scrub the surface walk the depths and dance
we harness heat water light and ultraviolet frequencies
to remain to appear to each other to love

it

is what

keeps keeping us here

MOURN (II)

Lament comes to me in other ways too – the tones of Shia suffering, drape black cloth for they killed Hossein[lxxiv] in Karbala, the pain re-learned, my pain now, Siavash before that before Hossein before me, year after year, but now especially

for grief is a timeloop, pain relived and re-enacted

on the streets now, chains slapping the back now, the chest now, razors across the forehead, the beating of the breast till blood, till the dripping from the liver, from the foot, from the sword, the gash, till tears, till pearls in the ocean, till the daughter of the prophet, till the mother of our master, till her name in every rain drop, till her infinite embrace, till her face of sun, and her face of moon

till martyr, till death, for the other, for you, for all, for this, till I am drained
of me, my blood at the end, till nothing, and nothing more
till then yes
I howl
how I howl
I moan
how I moan

Eight billion people out there in the world so indifferent
to your death

it makes the calamity around here not a scrub smaller

a hundred billion humans come and gone so far
since humans first stood up and walked
to the ends of the world—
what are they to me?
and who?

at what remove does my indifference start?

what are you to me?

In our millions in our billions
we are all Palestinians.

The mothers with white panuelos
refusing the remains of their disappeared
circling the plaza.
The wound they said will not close
until everyone... not just mine or me, until everyone not just us and ours, until everyone meaning until justice...[lxxv]
for this wound is not only my wound
so every time someone says their names,
the dead echo back. Presente.

Who hears the dead?
whose dead do **you** hear calling back?

a sign on the community garden across from Greenwood Cemetery
reads:

not a minute of silence for our dead
but a lifetime of struggle

so many lifetimes of struggle on the red soil
of nations   citizens of a wound[lxxvi]
gaping at a world that does not want to look screaming in a world that
does not want to hear marching in a world that does not want to be
disturbed where you need a million people and a banner to claim the
basics—Black Lives Matter—until then until everyone until Black we
live in the White gash across the world's chest
the ocean's   the sky's 

no ship water- or space-faring can cross

until then we mourn in this world to rearrange its absences

—in the wreckage[lxxviii]   find power

reappear[lxxvii]

UTTERANCE

On her first anniversary she said:
"The film is good."

On her second anniversary she said:
"Stop eating meat."

On her 3rd anniversary she said:
"The dead are not a plaything—
find out for yourself
where meaning ends."

On her fourth anniversary she said:

My 470000000000000000000000000000001 hydrogen protons

are everywhere

can you feel them?

Kiss my ghost.

PRESENCE

where are you where have you been
how are you where you have been
where are you now when you are not here
when is now where there is no now now is nothing
now is so long you have been away so long
so forsakenly long

this is long this is long already so fucking long how long will it be
when now is no different from eternity

the time of your disappearance
is everywhere all at once

she resides in the earth waiting have you not spoken to her?
she rekindles the stars at night have you not seen her?
she closes doors you leave open have you not felt her?
she flaps her white owl wings through the corridors have you not sighted her?
she rides along the horizon humming the future on her horse have you not heard her?
she carries the smell of the first rain on her dust have you not smelled her?
she was eaten up by the earth and regenerated have you not tasted her?

Someone having noticed the meds in the fridge
mentioned her morphine
and the oven dish exploded
right out of my hands
under yet another snowfall
on her anniversary and I was
left standing there with my empty mitts
the glass reverting to sand
scattered protons
the early universe reconstellated
on the kitchen floor...

really, this is no time for myth.
Naomi was there—she can tell you.

The absence of the dead is never trivial
neither is their presence
announced lightly

reality can shatter[lxxix]

in the way that

only reality
can shatter
this appearance.

this appearance

takes more work perhaps
when you are here—when one is—when I am

in disappearance

she has her own
stretches of this fabric to fold
wrinkles in the weave to disappear into
spinning all those elsewheres
in her freedom to not appear

reappearances are rare
the asymmetry feels unfair
it's hard work trying to reach enough of her

you enter jumbled time
the anesthetized dome[lxxx] breaks open
the nervous system unplugs
paint your nails breathe deep extend your hearing
stick needles into your flesh
learn to read the braille on your skin
    when they move
    learn to move with them as they move through
feel your electric differential, ride the continuum of being
    even as the amplitudes might recede

be prepared to receive not read
the signs and above all
be ready to give up
your seat

Do you feel the loneliness of the living?

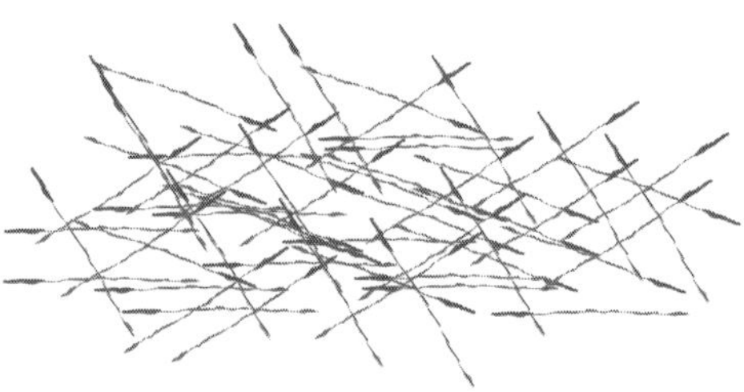

Or do you know how to shimmy with the dead?

PRESENCE (AGAIN)

The bark was brittle still and the cardinal's song out
of season,
the air came through in slices, chilled
from the cracked window

and
because I am like the window cracked
or because my breath like winter air slices
through my open chest,

I decide to re-launch Skype and try her.

Or
I don't know what I was thinking except this is another medium
through which we related, and that's all what I have left, ways, as many
as possible,
to reach into the plasmasphere.

Most likely I didn't think
no one thinks doing these kinds of things
until the dead backflip into this here-and-now.

It was the night of February 26
I closed the window
opened the laptop
got on to Skype.

aboufarman 2/26/2016 10:49:00 PM hi chups—i miss you

aboufarman 2/26/2016 10:49:10 PM every time i walk down these damned steps i think of you

aboufarman 2/26/2016 10:49:15 PM you know why

aboufarman 2/26/2016 10:49:29 PM you know what these steps mean

aboufarman 2/26/2016 10:49:37 PM but also for other reasons

aboufarman 2/26/2016 10:50:16 PM i see your decisions

aboufarman 2/26/2016 10:50:30 PM in every corner, and your eye

aboufarman 2/26/2016 10:50:45 PM i'm not well

aboufarman 2/26/2016 10:51:12 PM and i don't have any-one to be not well with

aboufarman 2/26/2016 10:51:18 PM come to me

aboufarman 2/26/2016 11:23:33 PM and you did!
you just did!

Notice time. Notice its lag.

At 10:51:18 I cry for your presence like someone crushed by your absence : come to me.

The next message comes 32 minutes later

the lag between death and life
where strangeness says hello.

At 10:51:19 I look up from the screen

a cockroach appears

from behind the Shipibo ceramic of you—and dances slowly up to the bed where I am propped up on those pillows, your fortress of pillows, and it tries to climb the metal nightstand.

I thought, it is so shiny, the nightstand, can it climb up?
But they that are of flesh mind the spirit and the spirit said, wait, let
no man deceive himself but I thought, really
are you coming to me, are you climbing this metal leg to me?

That is when it flapped and flew. This is a stunt, I thought.

Onanyas taught us that if any creature appears on your path or in your head you must not be afraid, you must immediately ask, who are you? And they will either tell you or they will slink away. I have asked this of a dog, a snake, an infected rat and an armed wanderer. I have asked this of trees and shadows on the street. I have asked this of my students. I ask this of myself.

I ask this of the cockroach

and she shimmies up to me
dances with her antennae
on the other side of time—

is this you?

is this me?

Ok, so, again, recap, on Skype
10:51:18 PM
come to me

[time gap—death gap—reappearance gap
-wherein all the above happened]

So I return 32 minutes later and write

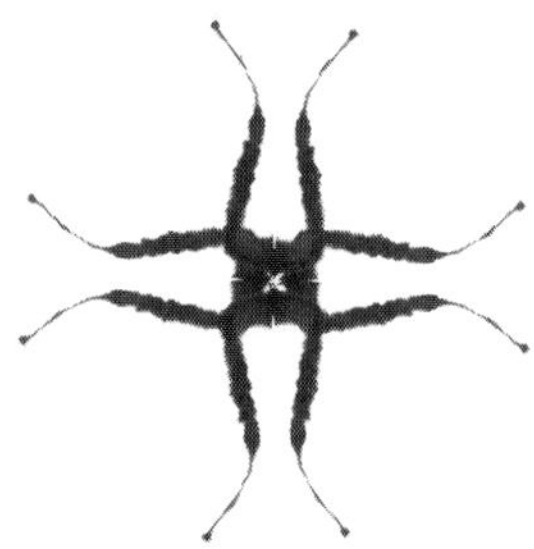

11:23:33 PM
and you did! you just did!

[cont'd]
aboufarman 2/26/2016 11:23:39 PM
after a long while—you came back
aboufarman 2/26/2016 11:24:22 PM
you as kafka as grygor as cockroach as metamorphosis
as your favorite
aboufarman 2/26/2016 11:24:35 PM
you just crawled across

aboufarman 2/26/2016 11:24:51 PM

under the bed to under the laundry container

aboufarman 2/26/2016 11:24:58 PM

after such a long time

aboufarman 2/26/2016 11:25:19 PM

and now to the shipibo lady

aboufarman 2/26/2016 11:26:13 PM

which is you too, another metamorphosis

aboufarman 2/26/2016 11:26:24 PM

your antennas are going wild around the shipibo lady

aboufarman 2/26/2016 11:26:27 PM

i sing to you yes i am singing to you

aboufarman 2/26/2016 11:26:40 PM

you move your antennae

aboufarman 2/26/2016 11:26:50 PM

you go behind the pot—where are yu now?

aboufarman 2/26/2016 11:27:03 PM

i know i can't keep you always here now

aboufarman 2/26/2016 11:27:36 PM

crawl across the wall

aboufarman 2/26/2016 11:27:42 PM

like an old cockroach

aboufarman 2/26/2016 11:28:11 PM

you came back young last month and now yu have aged

aboufarman 2/26/2016 11:29:06 PM

whom can

i
tell
these things
to?

Where meaning ends

acts of re-appearance occur repeatedly
an event as ordinary as speciation, as birth
a grandfather putting in a re-appearance
in the newborn

shards of the universe   cutting through the motherskin

another sun   rising   on another   fucking day
another damned night descending
another you another me
another time
another place
there was a cockroach

out of nothing   anything is excess
us finding form
needing to
at first
then needing   to drop it

creation runs through both
and mourning too

forms that have no name or measure[lxxxi]
because they came together on the other side of it all
before wave became sound
before sound became word
before word became feeling
before hearts could break
before anything had begun
or come to mean anything else
the unsung, and in it deep the song
the uncried, and the cry out of it
better at any rate to not call this song it is not for singing don't call
this song it is the infrawave of being don't call this song it is the
creature plants the teacher plants the mother plants the warrior plants
the worker plants rising up
don't call it song
it is the rising up
this unravelling back into and up from our hollow
each being emanating its own electromagnetic genius
wave upon wave resonating with yellow
with berry with chirisanango with toë with chuchuasi
with anaconda ant crabapple spider
web upon web spinning the unspun thinness of air
all gathered here buzzing like gods   like cockroaches
in the basement of transmutation

returning the extravagance of the sun
8-minute-old frequencies
pulsing the photosensitive soul
            every image a ghost given up
                        every ghost an image given off

you
your body
rose
and released
out of the Amazon
where you said life grows on every surface[lxxxi]
and in what you said
there was awe and envy, and understanding
the fullness of 390 billion trees
the canopy of dark biodiversity, hidden
unseen unknowable uncountable undiscoverable incurable
indeterminate occult life
still here four billion years later, never gone
never
eliminated exterminated extinct
but dying all the time all the same
every animalcule in the rainwater
every frog, turtle, bamboo rat, tunchi, paiche, anaconda, jaguar, toucan, ysango, dust mite, you, 99% of all species ever, everything dying all the damned time
and life
just keeps on being life, cellular circadian lit
but returning to darkness

—seeds, eggs, pods, wombs, caves these darknesses life breaks out of and goes back into, nightly, seasonally, perennially

regeneration   the source   is lightless   reimmersion
the source is always lightless, under the canopy below the spring
the cave the hole corpus cavernucum, never can the source be seen,
known, for how else can it become itself, arise into its own being
undetermined   surprising   becoming

you

and you

and you

and you

spin proton spin

PRAISE FOR *NO SILENCE IN THE AFTERLIFE*

n these searingly beautiful pages, an Orphic Abou Farman nixes euphemism and dissects cancer—molecularly and ontologically ("a tumor is . . . mutants in mutiny refusing death")—while daring to look back and retrace his partner Leonor Caraballo's deathmatch with the disease, which might as well be his deathmatch with her unmitigated absence. Tragically victorious through language, he transmutes his loss into the heartbreaking perfection of this elegiac work.

—MÓNICA DE LA TORRE, winner of the FCA C.D. Wright Award for Poetry '22, Brooklyn College

What happens when a heartbeat is no longer a sign of life but a measure counting down time left? A "turn in life" requires a new language. *No Silence in the Afterlife* is a book about love in the limited time of cancer. Farman's writing about his loss is ferocious yet gentle, funny and tragic, knee-deep in the visceral but concerned with the cosmic. It will change the way you think about loved and dying bodies, selves, and the afterlife.

—LISA STEVENSON, J. I. Staley Prize-winning author and anthropologist, McGill University

END

NOTES

APPEARING

DISAPPEARING

REAPPEARING

APPEARING

i

In the beginning was the strong nuclear force
binding three quarks
into a proton
so the universe got going . . .

Bogdan Povh et al., *Particles and Nuclei: An Introduction to the Physical Concepts*, 7th edition (Berlin, Heidelberg: Springer, 2015).

ii

". . . their persistent refusal to come out in the open
—to show themselves in our particle detectors—
was troubling... quarks [were] able to explain mounds of experimental
data without possessing
any 'innate' reality as objects of human experience.
Who could believe, after all, in something that
absolutely refused to reveal itself?"

Michael Riordan, *The Hunting of the Quark: A True Story of Modern Physics* (Lexington: Plunkett Lake Press, 2019).

iii

The word quark was invented by James Joyce in
Finnegan's Wake to approximate a seabird's call.

"Quark," in New World Encyclopedia, https://www.newworldencyclopedia.org/entry/quark.

iv

“A few millionths of a second later
[after the big bang],
quarks aggregated to produce protons and neutrons.
Within minutes, these protons and neutrons combined
into nuclei.”

Then, for a while, the universe didn’t do very much.
It took “380,000 years for electrons to be trapped
in orbits around nuclei, forming
the first atoms.”

The first we, two things revolving around each other.

“The Early Universe,” Conseil Européen
pour la Recherche Nucléaire,
https://home.cern/science/physics/early-universe.

vi

". . . use the word 'attraction' in general
for any endeavor whatever made by bodies
to approach each other,
whether that endeavor arise from the action
of the bodies themselves, as tending to each other
or agitating each other by spirits emitted;
or whether it arises from the action of the ether
or of the air,
or of any medium whatever, whether
corporeal or incorporeal
any how impelling bodies placed therein
toward
each other . . ."

Isaac Newton. *Prinicpia, Mathematical Principles of Natural Philosophy*, translated in Jourdain, Philip E. B. 2015.
Newton's Hypotheses of Ether and of Gravitation
From 1679 To 1693, The Monist , APRIL 1915, Vol. 25, p. 238

v

Another of the primordial forces is the
electromagnetic,
"transferred between charged particles through
the exchange of massless, force-carrying bosons
called photons, which are also the particle
components of light. The force-carrying photons
that swap between charged particles, however,
are . . . virtual and undetectable, even though they
are technically the same particles as the real
and detectable version."
Experts in the invisible say photons "have

no electric charge, no color, no strangeness,
charm, topness, or bottomness . . . "
But they have spin.
And can act instantly at infinite distance.

Jeremy Rehm, "The Four Fundamental Forces of Nature," *Livescience*, October 1, 2019, https://www.livescience.com/the-fundamental-forces-of-nature.html.

John Thacker, "The Four Forces: Range and Force Carriers," Duke University Department of Physics, January 29,1995, https://webhome.phy.duke.edu/~kolena/modern/forces.html.

vii

What feels spooky to physicists is not separation but entanglement—when photons that have come into contact remain under each other's influence forevermore such that a change in the state of one will affect the other instantly no matter how far they have separated in the meantime.

Davide Castelvecchi and Elizabeth Gibney, "'Spooky' Quantum Entanglement Experiments Win Physics Nobel," *Nature* 610 (October 2022): 214-242.

viii

In forever there is no meantime.

x

Freedom is unpredictability, lawlessness.
The future is freedom.

Nicholas Rescher. 1997. *Predicting the Future: An Introduction to the Theory of Forecasting.* SUNY Press.

xi

From another angle, to see the future is truly to foresee misfortune.

Susan Reynolds Whyte. *Questioning Misfortune: The Pragmatics of Uncertainy in Eastern Uganda.* (Cambridge: Cambridge University Press, 1997)

xii

Prognosis, writes Hippocrates, is the physician's art of "foreseeing what is to happen from the present state of matters," which comes down to "seeing and announcing beforehand those who will live and those who will die."

Hippocrates. 1868. "Prognostikon." In *The Genuine Works of Hippocrates.* Translated and edited by Charles Darwin Adams. (New York: Dover, 1939).

xiii

"Never is the future
Because tomorrow never comes
Comes tomorrow never...

The light of the future casts the shadow of tomorrow..."

SunRa, "Shadow of tomorrow" and "Never is the future," In *The Immeasurable Equation, The Collected Poetry and Prose*, eds James L. Wolf and Harttnut Geerken. (WAiT A WHILE Books, 2005)

xiv

At 3 o'clock. That is where the tumor is.
Oncologists use the hands of a clock to mark the geography of cancer around the breast. This is disconnected from the fact that a clock is used to tell the time. Tell the time, as in two years left.

xv

“Disease is the body losing
its innocence.”

Michel Foucault, preface to *The Normal and the Pathological*, by George Canguilheme, trans. Carolyn R. Fawcett, (New York: Zone Books, 1978).

xvi

“. . . they are even of opinion that they would never
die at all if it were not for the maleficent arts
of sorcerers who cut the vital thread prematurely
short. In other words, they disbelieve in what
we call a natural death; they think that all men
are naturally immortal in this life, and that every
death which takes place is in fact a violent death
inflicted by the hand of a human enemy, though
in many cases the foe is invisible.”
But to dismiss the idea
by saying death is merely natural
is to assume the universe innocent.

James George Frazer, *The Belief in Immortality and the Worship of the Dead, Volume I,* (London: Macmillan, 1913). XX

ix

A small change in one place,
say a butterfly flapping its wings in Texas, must
eventually down the chain contribute to some
large changes, say devastating tornados, in another
place, say Brazil. And maybe the other way
around too. There are so many small events—so
many butterfly wings flapping—that the future as

a complex whole can only be unpredictable. This
was theorized by a meteorologist when physics
was becoming entangled with weather forecasting
to give us chaos theory and poetry—two different
zones of freedom.

The butterfly effect is a different way of saying
we are entangled.

Edward Lorenz, "The Butterfly Effect," in *The Chaos Avant-garde: Memories of the Early Days of Chaos Theory*, ed. Ralph Abraham and Yoshisuke Ueda, (Singapore: World Scientific Publishing Co., 2000), 91-94.

xvii

Every body in the universe emanates
electromagnetic fields that affect other fields,
for "all life exists in a sea of EMFs."

David Cohen, "Magnetic Fields of the Human Body," Physics Today 28, no. 8 (August 1975): 34-43.

David Muehsam and Carlo Ventura, Life Rhythm as a Symphony of Oscillatory Patterns: Electromagnetic Energy and Sound Vibration Modulates gene Expression for Biological Signaling and Healing, *Global Adv Health Med.* 2014;3(2):40-55.

Your electromagnetic energy can
change gene expression, cause disorders,
it can also help heal, affect neuronal
connections and increase pain thresholds.

In our electromagnetic appearance on this Earth
we alter the sea
and are in turn altered in untold many
ways by each and every other appearance.

xviii

In one research project, scientists found human subjects
who emanated 1000 times the magnetic energy of
average humans. They attributed it to Qi energy
or the vital force.

A Seto et al., "Detection of Extraordinary Large Bio-Magnetic Field Strength from Human Hand During External Qi Emission," *Acupuncture and Electrotherapeutic Research* 17, no. 2 (1992): 75-94.

xx

Energy can also kill you.

xxi

And science too, handmaiden of war.

xxix

The "hiss" they heard
was of extraterrestrial origin.
Galactic radio, cosmic noise.
The WWII microwave radar specialist
who got to studying heavenly objects
through radio frequencies showed

these were emissions by hydrogen protons
in outer space. The image of the Milky Way
is now made not by eyes looking
but by instruments detecting the radio hiss
of galactic hydrogen.
Medical technologies that image the
interior of the body use the hydrogen proton's
radio waves too. Making images of inner space
and outer space depend on the same fundamental
technologies of the universe, little protons
radiating, saying hiss, saying hi.

Woodruff T. Sullivan, III, *Cosmic Noise: A History of Early Radio Astronomy,* (Cambridge: Cambridge University Press, 2009).

xxii

Protons radiate differently in the heart than
in the bone or in the lungs, the liver, veins,
stomach, muscle, breast, regular and cancer tissue.
All their important aspects—their charge, their magnetic
energy, their spin, their rhythm, their speed, their
history—is affected by their environment.
They behave differently depending on where they
end up—in water, in fat, in malady, in health,
in the pampas, at ground zero, in joy, in misery,
in alcohol, in morphine, in mourning, in
madness, on mushrooms, on ativan, in the brain,
in silicon. The speed at which they flip back
from a magnetically charged energy state into
their regular one is called their relaxation

rate: in water they relax fast, in your
tumors slow.

Donald W. McRobbie et al.,
MRI from Picture to Proton,
(Cambridge: Cambridge University Press, 2006).

xxiii

One of the first scientists who put these
observations to practical use, Armenian physician
and inventor of the Magnetic Resonance Imaging
(MRI) machine, wrote of his discoveries: "I had
been away from Him for some time having
embraced a godless theory of origins and even
seriously questioned God's very existence . . .
But though I had forgotten Him, He had not
forgotten me."

Jeff Kinley and Raymond Damadian, Gifted Mind:
*The Dr. Raymond Damadian Story, Inventor
of the MRI*, (Arkansas: New Leaf Publishing
Group, 2015).

xxv

The first nuclear image of the interior of the human
body was produced in 1977. It was of a finger.
Today, more than 100 million images of the insides
of humans are being produced every year
generating an economy of interior images worth
over $100 billion.
Are we seeing too much
or are we seeing too little?

A new condition of visibility is a new condition
of politics.

Robert R. Edelman, "The History of MR Imaging
as Seen Through the Pages of Radiology,"
Radiology 273, supp 2 (2014): supp 181-200.

xxiv

And if certain photoreceptors are hit with the right part of the color spectrum you can enhance your sleep cycles, improve cellular functioning and optimize cognition, all of it originating 93 million miles away. According to some chronobiologists, our circadian rhythms are linked to the motion of the planets, connecting interior and exterior temporalities through the electromagnetic field and we are still rocked to sleep by those very planetary motions and our cellular functions optimized by those same deep histories, by the frequencies of outer space, by the synaesthetic spectrum of the electromagnetic field.

A Farman. Introduction to synaesthetics.
The Senses and Society, (20(2), (2025): 222-230.

xxvi

When hydrogen protons fuse together
they produce, amongst other things, energy and
explosions
and that is all what the sun is
and light its paradox.

Marcelo Gleiser, "The Paradox of Light
Goes Beyond Wave-Particle Duality," *Big Think*,
https://bigthink.com/13-8/quantum-nature-of-light/.

DISAPPEARING

xxvii

Light is a packet of energy, photons from the sun.
When we receive light, a protein called opsin changes shape
triggering a chain of electrochemical signals
that become vision.
Photons land on opsins and we see things.
Not only see, sense.
Photoreceptors—including those on the skin
maybe on hair follicles too and the
pineal gland—affect our circadian rhythm, our moods, our magnetic
field, our sense of time.
Cellular functions optimize: we wake, we think,
we move, we flip in the generosity of the sun.

Mark S. Rea et al., "A Model of Phototransduction by the Human Circadian System," *Brain Research Reviews* 50, (2005): 213-228.

xxviii

Sunlight can damage DNA too, but if we evolve the right receptors it can heal. Early multicellular beings avoided irradiation by going deep into the ocean during daytime. There they evolved blue-light photoreceptors, since only a blue light frequency can penetrate deep into an aquatic environment. These photoreceptors allowed them to know when the night came on and when it was safe to come out of the water. The blue light photoreceptors also get involved in DNA repair to counter the damage caused by UV from sunlight. Hence an early evolutionary relationship grew between blue light photoreception, circadian rhythmicity and healing.

Walter Gehring and Michael Rosbash. The coevolution of blue-light photoreception and circadian rhythms. *Journal of Molecular Evolution* 2003; 57 Suppl 1:S286-9.

xxix

Plants don't use light to see. They have pigment
molecules, like chlorophyll, that get excited
when photons from the sun hit them.
Their electrons break free and gather
in the plant's reaction center. Then, as they drink water,
plants break down H2O, sending the hydrogen protons over to join
the electrons where, conjoined differently, they turn it all into
sugar. And that remaining oxygen atom is released
into the atmosphere.

Trees eat the sun, break down the water, and we breathe.

Shannon Brescher Shea, "Photosynthesis: Gathering Sunshine with the World's Smallest Antennas," Office of Science, November 3, 2016, https://www.energy.gov/science/articles/photosynthesis-gathering-sunshine-worlds-smallest-antennas.

lx

Once upon a time, there was almost no oxygen.
But there was life.
Anaerobic bacteria metabolised without
oxygen, held an exchange with a different kind of air.
Oxygen was the waste product. Over
a billion years all that waste product transformed
the Earth's atmosphere into an oxygenated one
allowing new forms of life to get going in that
fresh air. The new atmosphere also killed off
existing species that had not evolved to breathe
in all that oxygen.
"Oxygen is poisonous . . . and probably
carcinogenic," writes James Lovelock, the
originator of Gaia theory, which proposes

our planet as a living organism, a holistic and
metabolic system constantly self-regulating
water
oxygen
hydrogen
sun
spin
wave
proton

Today, We are in an era of "oxygen deficit."
Humans are rearranging the Earth's
atmosphere in all kinds of ways and the big
change won't take a billion years.

James Lovelock, *Gaia*, (Oxford: Oxford University Press, 1979).
Jianping Huang et al., "The Global Oxygen Budget and Its Future Projection," *Science Bulletin* 63, no. 18 (September 2018): 1180-1186.

xxxiv

"The back of this sky that fell in the beginning of time is now the forest where we live and the ground that we walk on. This is why we call the forest wãro patarima mosi, the old sky, and the shamans also call it hutukara, which is the name of this ancient celestial layer. Later another Sky came down and fixed itself above the Earth, replacing the one that had collapsed."

Davi Kopenawa and Bruce Albert. *The Falling Sky.* (Harvard University Press 2013), 131..

xxx

The Amazon is the name we give to the largest concentration of trees in the world. According to mathematical models, The Amazon Rainforest is constituted by more than 400 billion individual trees, the densest pool of carbon in the universe. In non-
mathematical models, 1.4 million hectares of trees
are being cut down every year.

Meelis Pärtel, Robert Szava-Kovats, and Martin Zobel, "Dark diversity: Shedding light on absent species," *Trends in Ecology and Evolution* 26, no. 3 (March 2011):124-128.

xxxi

Biologists have identified over 40,000 different plant
species, with 16,000 different tree species, 1,300 bird, and a few thousand mammal, reptile and amphibian species in the Amazon - ten percent of the Earth's known plant and animal species. Yet that accounts for only 3% of all species that must exist in the rainforest. Most of what's there is life undectetable by our instruments, absent to our experience.

Scientists have come to call this unseen mass "dark diversity."

Hans ter Steege et al., "Hyperdominance in the Amazonian Tree Flora," *Science* 342, no. 6156 (October 2013).

Mónica R. Moraes et al., "Biodiversity and Ecological Functioning in the Amazon," A*mazon Assessment Report 2021* (New York: United Nations Sustainable Development Solutions Network), https://www.doi.org/10.55161/IKRT9380.

xxxii

Life is always "making a difference between past and present; life binds time, expanding complexity and creating new problems for itself."

Lynn Margulis and Dorion Sagan, *What Is Life?*, (Berkeley: University of California Press, 2005), 86.

xlvi

" . . . a substantial part of any mountain formation consists in the debris of living beings but perhaps the same thing holds true for the cloud layer manipulated by marine micro-organisms."

Bruno Latour, *Facing Gaia*, (Cambridge: Polity Press, 2017), 93.

xlvii

There are 13 times more dead Homo sapiens today than living ones. Since we got up on our feet and wandered out of Africa, over 100 billion humans have come to live and die. Over 8 billion humans are alive today, more than at any point in the known history of the planet. But they will all die, just as all other beings born into the world have died. Just yesterday 155,000 human beings died.

Carl Haub, "How Many People Have Ever Lived on Earth?," Population Reference Bureau, November 15, 2022, https://www.prb.org/articles/how-many-people-have-ever-lived-on-earth/

xlv

For the greatest and only poet of the Republic of Sharangestan, the liver is the organ of history.

Before he lost his lungs in Montreal, Hossein
Sharang sang a lament called "Dripping From the
End" or "Meechekad az payan," in which the liver
metabolized the end times, overwhelmed, oozing
with toxicity, ruin and sorrow, dripping with
blood, interminably processing the catastrophe
of human history, heralding no new beginnings.

Hossein Sharang, *Le Livre Sauvage*,
(Montreal: Le Noroît, 2009).

xliv

"The Indian problem," they called it in the
backrooms of modernity where they felt
the problem was not disappearing naturally as predicted.
Under the aegis of a reproductive health and family planning initiative
launched in 1996 by the regime of
Alberto Fujimori, the Peruvian government chose
to deal with that problem by sterilizing 272,028
mostly Indigenous women, by removing their
ovaries without consent.

To disappear the next generation
at the pre-mother stage.

Alejandra Ballón, *Memorias del caso Peruano de esterilización forzada*,
(Lima: Biblioteca Nacional del Perú, 2014).

xlix

The calculated number of heartbeats within a lifetime among mammals plotted against life expectancy and body weight are, within an order of magnitude, remarkably constant. Mammals average somewhere around 1.5 billion heartbeats/lifetime. But mammals die at

different ages, some live shorter, some much longer, even if the number of heartbeats is on average more or less the same over their lifespan. That difference has to do with enerfy expenditure and is correlated with size: large animals live slow, have sluggish heartbeats and grow older, small animals live fast, have rapid heart rates, and die young. An elephant's heartbeats 30 times a minute, a mouse's 500 times. An elephant's life expectancy is about 60 years, whereas a mouse lives about 2 years. Humans are an outlier on this graph.

Levine HJ. Rest heart rate and life expectancy. *Journal of the American College of Cardiology.* 1997 Oct;30(4):1104-6.

Geoffrey West. *Scale: The Universal Laws of Life, Growth, and Death in Organisms, Cities, and Companies.* (Penguin Books, 2018).

lvii

"I decided I would take up the subject of lactation. . . . Accordingly I commenced to work at it, getting all the practical information I could about it from the farmers and the shepherds round. . . . I learnt this very remarkable fact, that is the custom in certain countries, to remove the ovaries of the cow after calving if it is wished to keep up the supply of milk. . . . This fact seemed to me of great interest, for it pointed to one organ holding the control over the secretion of another and separate organ. . . . I thought I might follow up on my old line of reasoning, and in cases of advanced carcinoma of the breast in young patients see what effects the removal of the tubes and ovaries would have on the progress of the cancerous growth." After the operation, "all vestiges of her precious cancerous disease had disappeared," reported the Scottish surgeon George Beatson. Thirty years later, a team of chemists from Imperial Chemical Industries would patent the chemical ICI46474 to treat infertility in women. The chemical had the opposite effect: it caused infertility. It did so by blocking the production of estrogen, a little like removing the ovaries chemically.

In the 1970s, the link between estrogen and breast cancer would get established. After clinical trials, ICI 46474 came on the market as the multi-billion dollar breast cancer fighting drug Tamoxifen.

George Thomas Beatson, "On the Treatment of Inoperable Cases of Carcinoma of the Mamma: Suggestions for a New Method of Treatment, with Illustrative Cases," *The Lancet*, 148 (3803), (July 18, 1896).

Amar Bhide, Srikant Datar, and Katherine Stebbins, "Tamoxifen -Reducing Breast Cancer Risks: Case Histories of Transformational Advances," Harvard Business School Accounting & Management Unit Working Paper no. 20-134 (August 2020).

lviii

"On January 20, 1845, Professor Louis Alexander Dugas of the Medical College of Georgia cut open an unnamed patient's breast to remove a malignant tumor. The patient underwent this surgery under the effects of mesmeric somnambulism and reported no pain. The operation was witnessed by five other medical men who confirmed their astonishment. Reports of painless surgery abound in the mid-19th century before the introduction of anesthetics. For example: "The whole breast, weighing sixteen ounces, with a tumor in it as large as a turkey's egg, was cut away and the wound was left open for about three quarters of an hour while six bleeding blood vessels were tied. . . .

The patient gave no indication whatsoever of sensation, but remained all the time in a sound mesmeric sleep. The placidity of her countenance was unaltered, the natural blush of her cheeks undiminished . . . "

The Zoist: A Journal of Cerebral Physiology and Mesmerism (April 1848).

xlviii

liv

Even though the authorities in charge after 9/11 kept saying the air was safe to breathe, studies of people exposed to the dust of collapse showed increased rates of cancer, including a number of men who developed breast cancer. "I didn't know that a male could get breast cancer," one man said.

Ananya Mandel, "Breast cancer cases among men who were at ground zero on 9/11
News-Medical, September 7, 201
https://www.news-medical.net/news/20180907/Breast-cancer-cases
among-men-who-were-at-ground-zero-on-911.asp

liii

"[one] hypothesis links the rise of antibiotic resistance in war settings to the toxic environmental legacies of war, which are

considerable in the case of Iraq. Scientific literature over the last two decades has shown links between heavy metal contaminants and the rapid development of resistance in
bacteria... From bombing campaigns, to sanctions, to full scale invasion, to the so-called War on Terror, Iraq has
been at the forefront of Western interventions over decades which have changed the very ecosystem in which people live.
In such a context, Iraqibacter may be the culmination of many things: the decades of militarization and wounding, the collapse of infection control and infrastructure, the
movement of the injured across the region to seek healthcare, the overuse and misuse of antibiotics driven by sanctions, the proliferation of poor-quality drugs and counterfeit medicines and the destruction and contamination of the natural and lived environment. All define a toxic legacy of decades of war that are endured in the wounds and bodies of Iraqis . . .
. . . What would it look like if we plot genetic kinship trees of bacteria onto a history of political events and changing healthcare practices?
. . . Unravelling the genetic life of bacteria in time and space would just begin to link the microbiological biographies with the biographies and ecologies of war and intervention."

Omar Dewachi, "From the Archive: Iraqibacter and the Pathologies of Intervention," *Middle East Report Online*, March 09, 2020.

lv

When US President Barack Obama assassinated Osama Bin Laden, thousands of American Yahoo! News readers, such as

Geo J The Nkp Fan Sat Jun 11, 2011 08:03 pm PDT Report Abuse, Chris Wed Jun 08, 2011 10:21 am PDT Report Abuse, Sowhat! Sat Jun 11, 2011 05:09 pm PDT Report Abuse,

responded in the mode of racist ecstasy, calling for the genocide of Muslims, Arabs, and various other kinds. After the US started its region-wide war based on fake news of Weapons of Mass Destruction in 2003, I collected similar genocidal rants on Yahoo! News. As per the prompts of Yahoo! News itself, I reported some of these posts as abusive. Nothing was done about any of it as they were merely echoes of George W. Bush's own words, who said that Afghans and Arabs are not human and don't appreciate life like the Americans do.

lvi

Two decades later, as the Israeli government got going with its genocidal war to eliminate Palestine, the defense minister, Yoav Gallant, echoed much of the same language from that time: "We are fighting human animals and we act accordingly."

Sanjana Karanth, "Israeli Defense Minister Announces Siege On Gaza To Fight 'Human Animals'," *Huff Post*, Oct 9, 2023, https://www.huffpost.com/entry/israel-defense-minister-human-animals-gaza-palestine_n_6524220ae4b09f4b8d412e0a

Decades earlier, Hannah Arendt asked, "What meaning has the concept of murder when we are confronted with the mass production of corpses?"

Hannah Arendt, *The Origins of Totalitarianism*, (New York: Schocken Books, 1958), 441.

lxxvi

He deserted his family
let grow his beard
and filled his solitude with rocks and mist
He arrived in the desert
head wrapped in a shroud
blood spilled
on occupied land
He was neither
hero nor martyr
just a citizen of the wound

Tahar Ben Jelloun, "Il Quitta Sa Famille,"
in *Les amandiers sont morts de leurs blessures*,
(Paris: Maspero, 1976). Poem translated by A Farman

li

From the Greek tragoedia, where oide means song
and tragos means goat, tragedy is a goat song.
Or, according to some , tragedy is a "killing the goat
song," a ritual engagement with sacrifice,
which is in the deepest sense, the problematic of survival:
how to live
when in order to live
we must take life.
As ritual, sacrifice placed killing outside life and
time so the living could live with it.

Hugh Lloyd-Jones, "Ritual and Tragedy," in
*The Further Academic Papers of Sir Hugh
Lloyd-Jones*, (Oxford: Oxford Academic, 2005).

lix

"... the moderation of violence is part of the very logic of violence."

Eyal Weizman, *The Least of All Possible Evils: Humanitarian Violence from Arendt to Gaza*, (London: Verso, 2012), 3-4.

lii

"The survivor exists as temporally dislocated from the collective ... "

S. Lochlan Jain, *Malignant: How Cancer Becomes Us*, (Berkeley: University of California Press, 2013), 32.

l

Evolution can't explain all our striving because it assumes it; in other words, evolution can't explain its own first assumption: survival.

lxi

Cells can only divide faithfully up to about 60 times before their mechanism for making correct copies of themselves breaks down. At that point, good cells commit apoptosis, a noble death. They kill themselves so that they don't make faulty cells. As those cells die off, we lose the ability to renew ourselves. We age.

Some cells refuse to die. Those cells become cancer cells. They become immortal. They make us mortal.

REAPPEARING

lxii

Protons are stable. No one has ever seen one decay into something else. Protons are called the only eternal thing in the universe.

Francis Matthew, "Do Protons Decay?," *Symmetry: Dimensions of Particle Physics* (September 22, 2015), https://www.symmetrymagazine.org/article/do-protons-decay?language_content_entity=und.

xxxvii

For the Desana people in the Colombian Amazon, it is not the presence of a thing to sight that matters. Rather, everything in the world leaves an echo, and "only by being able to 'hear that echo' can one truly know what is being seen and what it symbolizes."

Gerardo Reichel-Dolmatoff, *Beyond the Milky Way: Hallucinatory Images of the Turkano Indians,* (Los Angeles: UCLA Latin American Center Publications, 1978), 152.

xli

Animal eyes evolved out of plant pigment cells.

Michael F. Land and Dan-Eric Nilsson, *Animal Eyes*, 2nd ed. (Oxford: Oxford University Press, 2012).

Vision is animal kingdom photosynthesis.
Or photosynthesis may be how plants see the world.

xxxvi

The old Ayahuasca healer Ino Moxo, who wandered as
much around the mind as around the jungle,
begins his cosmological teachings with this question: "What do you
hear when you listen to the jungle?"

The answer that unfolds across 270 pages:
The Mind of the Jungle
The Jungle of the Mind

César Calvo, *Three Halves of Ino Moxo: Teachings of the Wizard of the Upper Amazon,* trans. Kenneth Symington, (Rochester: Inner Traditions, 1995).

xxxviii

Awe for all we see when we can see.
Equal awe for all we see when we can't see.

Alkaloids in the ayahuasca vine allow DMT
molecules from the sister chacruna plant to
go from the guts to the brain's reaction center
creating visions in the dark.

We see without light, for the sun also is in our minds
photosynthesized by neurons and plant alkoloids.

Débora González et al., "Therapeutic Potential of Ayahuasca in Grief: a Prospective, Observational Study," *Psychopharmacology* 2 37, no. 4 (2020): 1171-1182.

xlii

When the Shipibo leader Ronald Suarez Maynas came to New York from the Amazon and went to Times Square, he stopped dreaming there were so many images.

xliii

One study showed that if you watch more black and white TV your dreams will come to you more in grayscale.

Nina Konig et al., "Colors in Dreams and the Introduction of Color TV in Germany," *International Journal of Dream Research* 10, no. 1 (April 2017): 59-64.

xl

In the West, hallucinations are thought of as visions out of control, rushing you without your consent. For Shipibo healers in the Amazon, visions are multilayered interactions with plant consciousness and the sphere of patterned forms that underlie existence.
Meaning not that in visionary activity you see what is not there to be seen, but rather the opposite: that in those regular times, you are failing to see what in reality is seeable.

Ralph Metzner, *Sacred Vine of Spirits: Ayahuasca*, (Rochester: Park Street Press, 2005).

xxxix

"For the real question is to know how it comes
that experience is not sufficient unto itself, but
presupposes certain conditions which are exterior
and prior to it . . .
Animals know only one world, the one which
they perceive by experience, internal as well as
external. Men alone have the faculty of conceiving
the ideal, of adding something to the real."

Emile Durkheim, *Elementary Forms of the Religious Life,* trans. Karen Fields, (New York: The Free Press, 1995), 15, 421.

lxiii

Orpheus is a literal tale about the feeling of one hand
in another.
The hand slips away from all of us who are trying
to hold it.
How do you keep on holding
while not holding on
to those who have died
their hands or kneecaps or bunions?
Orpheus sang and cried.
You?

lxiv

There is no clear evolutionary explanation for
crying, but one theory holds that humans cry
because we appear in the world helpless and

dependent. Crying is the first adaptation, it makes
us fit for survival. We cry to not die, to not get
killed. Later, perhaps, we cry to not kill
ourselves. We break down, exude water and live on.

Michael Trimble, *Why Humans Like to Cry*, (Oxford: Oxford University Press, 2012).

lxvii

In proper mourning, your eyes must run like rivers. "Tears at the grave
nourish and water the dead
and slake their thirst . . . to quench the thirst of
the dead is to bestow memory upon them."

Gay Ord Pollock Lynch, "Why Do Your Eyes Not Run Like a River? Ritual Tears in Ancient and Modern Greek Funerary Traditions," in *Holy Tears: Weeping in the Religious Imagination*, eds. Kimberley Christine Patton and John Stratton Hawley, (Princeton: Princeton University Press, 2016).

lxxiii

"Since the human body contains the cosmos,
its destruction through fire and water [in the River
Ganges] is both a repetition of the conflagration
and inundation of the cosmos and the end of
time and a prelude to its regeneration."

Jonathan Parry, "The End of the Body," in *Fragments for a History of the Human Body, Part Two,* ed. Jonathan Crary et al., (New York: Zone Books, 1989), 503.

lxv

Life is an activity that maintains wetness in an ongoing exchange with sky and plants.

Lynn Margulis and Stephen Harding, *Animate Earth: Science, Intuition and Gaia*, (White River Junction: Chelsea Green Publishing, 2006).

lxvi

"There is the idea that the path of the stars is nothing more than the continuation of the rivers. The rivers continue. What we call the Milky Way is a great river. The wente mapu, the world above, and the world below, the underworld: these three dimensions are intertwined; they cross paths and trace paths that have to do with our own life. It is not just burying a being. We are also weaving together those three dimensions."

Moira Ivana Millán. In The Earth's Remembrance, A Conversation between Moira Ivana Millán and Jean-Daniel Lafontant, *Critical Times*, December 2023, 6:3, 414.

lxviii

"Tears at the grave nourish and water the dead and slake their thirst . . . to quench the thirst of the dead is to bestow memory upon them."

Gay Ord Pollock Lynch, "Why Do Your Eyes Not Run Like a River? Ritual Tears in Ancient and Modern Greek Funerary Traditions," in Holy Tears: Weeping in the Religious Imagination, eds. Kimberley Christine Patton and John Stratton Hawley, (Princeton: Princeton University Press, 2016).

lxxiv

The prophet's grandson Hossein was martyred
in the desert of Karbala where tears were the only
water left. Our millenialist legacy: a bloody battle,
a parched land, a weeping cosmos. This Shia cosmology both accounts
for the movement of history
—as an on-going battle against usurpation—and
provides the required affective triggers for feeling
the pain of others and generate outrage against
injustice. Crying reminds you to take on those
duties.

lxix

The formal act of crying is part of a lengthy
process that is triggered upon the death of a leader
in Ondo-Yoruba towns. Formal crying is also part
of marriage ceremonies because if marriage is
a union, a coming together, it is one that entails a
departure too.

Jacob Olupona and Sola Ajibade, "EnkuńÌyàwó: Bridal Tears in Marriage Rites of Passage among the`Yorùbá of Nigeria," in *Holy Tears: Weeping in the Religious Imagination*, (Princeton: Princeton University Press, 2016).

lxx

"The body of the mourner, the dying person, or
the dead are margins between self and society, life
and death, and function as places of mediation."

Nadia Seremetakis, *The Last Word: Women, Death, and Divination in Inner Mani,* (Chicago: University of Chicago Press, 1991).

lxxi

English anthropologist Alfred Radcliffe-Brown's account of weeping amongst Andaman Islanders from the 1920s describes crying as the proper emotional response upon embracing a friend after a long time apart. In recognition of separation, tears also become a medium of reattachment.

A.R. Radcliffe-Brown, *The Andaman Islanders*, (Cambridge: The University Press, 1906).

lxxii

Kaluli have experts so powerful in mourning work that not only does their singing and dancing elicit tears from the bereaved but, according to the ethnographer Edward Schieffelin, the depth of suffering induced had to be so profound, so real, that the grieving relative would want to grab a torch and jam it into the performer's shoulder. To mourn well is to burn the performer in rage, in pain, and in revenge for the suffering and the burning the performance had made them relive, just as though this were the original pain and that was not a performer.

The act of burning and being burnt,
the act of mourning, is a practice to
engage the pain of the world, not to erase it.

Edward Schieffelin, *The Sorrow of the Lonely and the Burning of the Dancers,* (London: Palgrave MacMillan, 2005).

lxxv

"When the body is freed (when day comes) it follows the explosive scream.

Since speech was forbidden, slaves camouflaged the word under the provocative intensity of the scream. No one could translate the meaning of what seemed to be nothing but a shout. It was taken to be nothing but the call of a wild animal. This is how the dispossessed man organized his speech by weaving it into the apparently meaningless texture of extreme noise. There developed from that point a specialized system of significant insignificance."

Édouard Glissant, "Poetics," in *Caribbean Discourse: Selected Essays*, trans. J. Michael Dash (Charlottesville: University Press of Virginia, 1989), 122–125

xxxv

Sound is the deformation of a medium; hearing is reformation.

xxxiii

Bats can hear frequencies over 100KHz. Pink dolphins in the Amazon can pick up 280 KHz. Human hearing falls below 20KHz and fails beyond. We miss so much. What happens to all that is not heard?

lxxvi

"Silent death is the bad death"

Nadia Seremetakis. *The Last Word.* (Chicago: University of Chicago Press, 1991), 76.

lxxvii

"But there is a lot happening underground. Not only coffins, but seeds, roots and rhizomes. And maybe even tunnels and other lines of flight to new worlds, where alternative forms of kinship have room to grow and to nourish other life forms and ways of living" so that "spiritual kin" may be called upon in the "fight against imperialist, white supremacist opponents… "

Ruha Benjamin. "Black AfterLives Matter: Cultivating Kinfulness as Reproductive Justice." In *Making Kin not Population*, eds. Adele Clarke and Donna Haraway, (Prickly Paradigm Press, 2018), 47.

lxxviii

". . . the term 'ghost' neither confirms nor denies the metaphysical. It simply invokes a framework in which terror and unpredictability, grief and unrest, guilt and injustice, ancestors and demons can be called upon to empower and liberate us, not from the fact that we have been violated or even that violation continues, but from a condition of inability to locate the heart and soul of the problem."

Viviane Saleh-Hanna. 2015. *Black Feminist Hauntology: Rememory or the Ghosts of Abolition?* Champ pénal/Penal field, Vol. XII | 2015.

lxxix

Ghosts are a kind of ontological refugee.

Heonik Kwon. *Ghosts of War in Vietnam.*
(Cambridge: Cambridge University Press, 2008), 16

lxxx

“Increasingly stronger stimuli are needed
to provide people in anaesthetic society
with any sense of being alive.”

Ivan Illich. *Medical Nemesis,*
(London: Calder and Boyers, 1975), 106.

lxxxi

Emptiness has no measure.

Giordano Bruno, *On the Infinite, the Universe and the Worlds: Five Cosmological Dialogues*, trans. Scott Gosnell, (Scotts Valley: CreateSpace Independent Publishing Platform, 2014).

GRATITUDES

A village!? It takes a whole universe. I extend my deep gratitude to all my friends who knowingly or not helped us, me and Leo, get through this—and on to the other side. I have learned so much from Julie Patton about life and improvisation, and how they must be one and the same; without your magic I would not have had performances, without you I would not have had the courage. Tonya Foster accompanied me in many writing sessions on and off zoom, my ear trained on hers, though so defectively. You helped me stand on the solid ground of your wisdom, and in the bigness of your love. If you can't take the criticism get out of this business—that is my relationship to Noreen Khawaja. The most complete, transformative and courageous comments came from your pen. You made me fall off my bike so I had to learn to walk again. Practices make perfect—Khokhoi showed me Butoh, massage therapy, ceremonies of gratitude, altar making, herbalist concoctions, play needles, decolonial kick-you-in-the-gluteus-maximus arts. Respect. KS Brewer protected me often in our larvae. Matteo Norzi wove well the Shipibo patterns of our afterlife. Shelby Coley always rolling the doubts into insight. Other writing friends gave me their comments which helped hone passages, but more than anything gave me their friendship, which helped me move right in my relations: Saretta Morgan, Christina Olivares, Amir Soltani, Debbora Battaglia.

Performances and presentations over the years have helped us gain access to each other and get to hone the performance texts, working alongside many spirits: Julie Patton, Tonya Foster, Sholeh Asgary, Tiffany Hsu, Danielle Gauthier, Shelby Coley, Kelsey Brewer, Matteo Norzi, Hossein Sharang, my students at the School of Criticism and Theory. I felt many of the feelings through movement in Diego Pinon's Butoh Ritual Mexicano and Jacquelyn Marie Shannon's ghostly practice. Always Ali Bahman. Always Miriam Ticktin. Tanya McKinnon and

Julian Samuel—my first teachers, who twisted my bourgeois ears into social listening. And Amir Naderi who disciplined me into art. Two winter stays at Millay Arts helped the text come together on the page. Beatriz and her santos gave me a line to the underworld (deep apologies to those who got hurt along the way—acknowledgments must acknowledge the harm, too) and thanks to Janet Valencia la bruja chistosa for cleaning all our souls and deepest spaces.

I am honored by the contribution made by the great Shipibo artist Sara Flores. She is brighter than the sun. Fiorella, her granddaughter, helped break up and re-pattern the work on the page. Isabel Arciniegas Guaneme helped the cockroach body fragment and reconstitute.

Leo thanks all the practitioners—doctors, healers, nurses, artists—who helped her find ways through the labyrinth of pain and uncertainty. She is afraid that she, too, at some point will have to love a ghost.